T0209411

An Analysis of

John Rawls's

A Theory of Justice

Filippo Dionigi
with
Jeremy Kleidosty

LONDON AND NEW YORK

Published by Macat International Ltd
24:13 Coda Centre, 189 Munster Road, London SW6 6AW.

Distributed exclusively by Routledge
4 Park Square, Milton Park, Abingdon, Oxon OX14 4RN
605 Third Avenue, New York, NY 10017

Routledge is an imprint of the Taylor & Francis Group, an informa business

Copyright © 2017 by Macat International Ltd
Macat International has asserted its right under the Copyright, Designs and Patents Act
1988 to be identified as the copyright holder of this work.

The print publication is protected by copyright. Prior to any prohibited reproduction, storage in
a retrieval system, distribution or transmission in any form or by any means, electronic, mechanical, recording or otherwise, permission should be obtained from the publisher or where
applicable a license permitting restricted copying in the United Kingdom should be obtained
from the Copyright Licensing Agency Ltd, Barnard's Inn, 86 Fetter Lane, London EC4A 1EN, UK.

The ePublication is protected by copyright and must not be copied, reproduced, transferred,
distributed, leased, licensed or publicly performed or used in any way except as specifically
permitted in writing by the publishers, as allowed under the terms and conditions under which
it was purchased, or as strictly permitted by applicable copyright law. Any unauthorised distribution or use of this text may be a direct infringement of the authors and the publishers' rights
and those responsible may be liable in law accordingly.

www.macat.com
info@macat.com

Cataloguing in Publication Data
A catalogue record for this book is available from the British Library.
Library of Congress Cataloguing-in-Publication Data is available upon request.
Cover illustration: Etienne Gilfillan

ISBN 978-1-912303-44-1 (hardback)
ISBN 978-1-912127-84-9 (paperback)
ISBN 978-1-912282-32-6 (e-book)

Notice
The information in this book is designed to orientate readers of the work under analysis,
to elucidate and contextualise its key ideas and themes, and to aid in the development
of critical thinking skills. It is not meant to be used, nor should it be used, as a
substitute for original thinking or in place of original writing or research. References and
notes are provided for informational purposes and their presence does not constitute
endorsement of the information or opinions therein. This book is presented solely for
educational purposes. It is sold on the understanding that the publisher is not engaged
to provide any scholarly advice. The publisher has made every effort to ensure that
this book is accurate and up-to-date, but makes no warranties or representations with
regard to the completeness or reliability of the information it contains. The information
and the opinions provided herein are not guaranteed or warranted to produce particular
results and may not be suitable for students of every ability. The publisher shall not be
liable for any loss, damage or disruption arising from any errors or omissions, or from
the use of this book, including, but not limited to, special, incidental, consequential or
other damages caused, or alleged to have been caused, directly or indirectly, by the
information contained within.

CONTENTS

THE MACAT LIBRARY

The Macat Library is a series of unique academic explorations of seminal works in the humanities and social sciences – books and papers that have had a significant and widely recognised impact on their disciplines. It has been created to serve as much more than just a summary of what lies between the covers of a great book. It illuminates and explores the influences on, ideas of, and impact of that book. Our goal is to offer a learning resource that encourages critical thinking and fosters a better, deeper understanding of important ideas.

Each publication is divided into three Sections: Influences, Ideas, and Impact. Each Section has four Modules. These explore every important facet of the work, and the responses to it.

This Section-Module structure makes a Macat Library book easy to use, but it has another important feature. Because each Macat book is written to the same format, it is possible (and encouraged!) to cross-reference multiple Macat books along the same lines of inquiry or research. This allows the reader to open up interesting interdisciplinary pathways.

To further aid your reading, lists of glossary terms and people mentioned are included at the end of this book (these are indicated by an asterisk [*] throughout) – as well as a list of works cited.

Macat has worked with the University of Cambridge to identify the elements of critical thinking and understand the ways in which six different skills combine to enable effective thinking.
Three allow us to fully understand a problem; three more give us the tools to solve it. Together, these six skills make up the **PACIER** model of critical thinking. They are:

ANALYSIS – understanding how an argument is built
EVALUATION – exploring the strengths and weaknesses of an argument
INTERPRETATION – understanding issues of meaning

CREATIVE THINKING – coming up with new ideas and fresh connections
PROBLEM-SOLVING – producing strong solutions
REASONING – creating strong arguments

To find out more, visit **WWW.MACAT.COM.**

CRITICAL THINKING AND *A THEORY OF JUSTICE*

Primary critical thinking skill: REASONING
Secondary critical thinking skill: EVALUATION

John Rawls's *A Theory of Justice* is one of the most influential works of legal and political theory published since the Second World War. It provides a memorably well-constructed and sustained argument in favour of a new (social contract) version of the meaning of social justice. In setting out this argument, Rawls aims to construct a viable, systematic doctrine designed to ensure that the process of maximizing good is both conscious and coherent – and the result is a work that foregrounds the critical thinking skill of reasoning. Rawls's focus falls equally on discussions of the failings of existing systems – not least among them Marxism and Utilitarianism – and on explanation of his own new theory of justice.

By illustrating how he arrived at his conclusions, and by clearly explaining and justifying his own liberal, pluralist values, Rawls is able to produce a well-structured argument that is fully focused on the need to persuade. Rawls explicitly explains his goals. He discusses other ways of conceptualizing a just society and deals with counter-arguments by explaining his objections to them. Then, carefully and methodically, he defines a number of concepts and tools—"thought experiments"—that help the reader to follow his reasoning and test his ideas. Rawls's hypothesis is that his ideas about justice can be universally applied: they can be accepted as rational in any society at any time.

ABOUT THE AUTHOR OF THE ORIGINAL WORK

Born in 1921, **John Rawls** was an American philosopher from an upper-middle-class Christian family. Two of his brothers died while he was a child. Then, as a soldier during World War II, he saw the horrific effects of the destruction of Hiroshima by nuclear bomb. Rawls returned to civilian life without his faith and with a belief that life was both short and unfair. But he also believed that human endeavor could make life fairer, and dedicated his career to studying justice. He died in 2002 at the age of 81.

ABOUT THE AUTHORS OF THE ANALYSIS

Dr Filippo Dionigi holds a PhD from LSE, where he is currently a Leverhulm Early Career Fellow in International Relations. He is the author of Hezbollah, Islamist Politics and International Society (Palgrave MacMillan, 2014).

Dr Jeremy Kleidosty received his PhD in international relations from the University of St Andrews. He is currently a postdoctoral fellow at the University of Jväskylä, and is the author of *The Concert of Civilizations: The Common Roots of Western and Islamic Constitutionalism*.

ABOUT MACAT

GREAT WORKS FOR CRITICAL THINKING

Macat is focused on making the ideas of the world's great thinkers accessible and comprehensible to everybody, everywhere, in ways that promote the development of enhanced critical thinking skills.

It works with leading academics from the world's top universities to produce new analyses that focus on the ideas and the impact of the most influential works ever written across a wide variety of academic disciplines. Each of the works that sit at the heart of its growing library is an enduring example of great thinking. But by setting them in context – and looking at the influences that shaped their authors, as well as the responses they provoked – Macat encourages readers to look at these classics and game-changers with fresh eyes. Readers learn to think, engage and challenge their ideas, rather than simply accepting them.

'Macat offers an amazing first-of-its-kind tool for interdisciplinary learning and research. Its focus on works that transformed their disciplines and its rigorous approach, drawing on the world's leading experts and educational institutions, opens up a world-class education to anyone.'

Andreas Schleicher
Director for Education and Skills, Organisation for Economic Co-operation and Development

'Macat is taking on some of the major challenges in university education … They have drawn together a strong team of active academics who are producing teaching materials that are novel in the breadth of their approach.'

Prof Lord Broers,
former Vice-Chancellor of the University of Cambridge

'The Macat vision is exceptionally exciting. It focuses upon new modes of learning which analyse and explain seminal texts which have profoundly influenced world thinking and so social and economic development. It promotes the kind of critical thinking which is essential for any society and economy.
This is the learning of the future.'

Rt Hon Charles Clarke, former UK Secretary of State for Education

'The Macat analyses provide immediate access to the critical conversation surrounding the books that have shaped their respective discipline, which will make them an invaluable resource to all of those, students and teachers, working in the field.'

Professor William Tronzo, University of California at San Diego

WAYS IN TO THE TEXT

KEY POINTS

- John Rawls (1921–2002) was one of the twentieth century's most influential American philosophers.

- Rawls served in the US military during World War II.* This experience led him to write extensively about issues related to justice and society.

- *A Theory of Justice* argues that societies should pursue "justice as fairness."* He encouraged people to imagine a theoretical society that would be perceived as fair by all social classes.

Who Was John Rawls?

John Rawls, the author of *A Theory of Justice* (1971), was born in 1921 in Baltimore, Maryland to an upper-middle-class Christian family. His father was a well-known lawyer and his mother was the local president of the League of Women Voters* (an organization with a largely progressive political agenda, originally founded to help women to claim a more active role in civic life).

As an undergraduate at Princeton University, Rawls was exposed to the ideas of the American philosopher Norman Malcolm.* Malcolm had been a pupil of the Austrian philosopher Ludwig Wittgenstein,* who was fascinated by the role that language plays in the way we think. This idea would feed into Rawls's later academic interest in the way societies define what they mean by the term "justice."

Rawls's Princeton years were characterized by a deeply religious approach to political philosophy.* He considered studying theology and entering the priesthood. But when Rawls was 20, the United States entered World War II. Two years later, Rawls was on active duty in the Pacific. His military experiences between 1943 and 1946 led him to reject his faith and to seek an alternative means of conceptualizing a good, or just, society.[1] Choosing political philosophy as the best means of realizing this goal, Rawls became an academic. He worked at the Massachusetts Institute of Technology (MIT) and Cornell University, before accepting a position at Harvard University in 1962.

In the decades before his death in 2002, John Rawls became one of the most influential and frequently cited political thinkers of his generation. His first book, *A Theory of Justice*, was published in 1971. This highly regarded work, inspiring debate, criticism, and widespread admiration, established his reputation as a political philosopher.

What Does *A Theory of Justice* Say?

John Rawls's aim in *A Theory of Justice* is to develop a new way for people to think about justice. He wants to offer an alternative to the ideas of utilitarian* philosophy. Utilitarianism argues that the morality of an action should be judged according to its consequences; a "virtuous" action achieves the greatest good for the greatest number of people. Utilitarian ideas were very popular at the time when Rawls was writing *A Theory of Justice*, but Rawls opposed them. He argues that utilitarianism ignores the wellbeing of the individual, considering only an action's benefit to the majority. This, says Rawls, opens the door to abuse and suffering.

To replace utilitarianism, Rawls revives the tradition of the social contract.* A key idea in the liberal* political tradition, with its emphasis on the importance of individual liberty, this is the idea that society is based on an implicit contract between the state and each citizen of that state. The agreement is that the individual will give up some of their natural freedoms (essentially, the freedom to do whatever they like, whenever they like), while, in exchange, the state will create a society that protects the individual.

Rawls's picture of society is a group composed of free and rational individuals with a sense of justice. This is an underlying assumption of his work. He argues that the members of this society—defined as "a cooperative venture for mutual advantage"[2]—would all agree on the principles that should underpin a just society. Rawls defines justice as fairness; for him, justice should rely on conditions and procedures that everyone regards as fair.[3] He is interested in justice as the foundation for the "basic structure" of society: core values embodied in core institutions.

Rawls argues that a truly just society is one that would be considered just by all of its members, regardless of their social class or religious or moral beliefs. As it is hard for any individual to imagine what a just society would look like from a perspective other than their own, Rawls provides tools (thought experiments*) to help his readers make this empathetic leap.[4] He also provides other ideas to help everyone reflect on social justice and what it means. These ideas include a concept that Rawls call "reflective equilibrium"*—the idea that people develop their understanding of justice by questioning and reevaluating until they reach a point of equilibrium.[5]

Rawls called another innovative concept the "difference principle."* He argues that unequal wealth can be tolerated in a just society if this inequality is beneficial to its least advantaged people; it may be socially beneficial, for example, to incentivize someone with the right abilities to spend time training to become a surgeon, as the work they would do would benefit society. But Rawls qualifies this argument by saying that the means of earning unequal wealth should come from jobs that are open to anyone on the basis of merit.[6]

The importance of Rawls's method lies in its claim to religious and cultural neutrality: all members of society should believe their society is fair. Rawls's unique approach sees people as inherently equal in worth, but recognizes that people have unequal abilities. Some people can contribute more to the good of society than others. And, finally, inequality may exist—even in a just society.

Why Does *A Theory of Justice* Matter?

Written in the tradition of liberal political theory, Rawls's work emphasizes the idea of universal human rights* and the importance of every individual human being. The key themes of *A Theory of Justice* are central pillars of the liberal tradition. They include justice, individual equality, liberty, and the importance of reason and public reasoning. And the political question he asks is a recurring one: how can people live the best life possible in a society that is best able to give all people a good life?

Some of the assumptions that Rawls makes, however, limit how his work is applied. *A Theory of Justice* was published in 1971. In the following decades, demands for justice became increasingly global in character, highlighting how deeply Rawls's theory was rooted in the Western liberal tradition. Rawls's theory of justice aims to be universal. He claims it can be universally derived and universally applied. But it is not well suited to discussing justice in international relations. Global poverty, just war, and tolerance are at the top of the global political agenda. While there is also debate about the principles that should regulate a just international society and what moral obligations people have towards those in other countries, these are issues only briefly addressed in Rawls's theory of justice. His work is primarily concerned with domestic democratic social institutions such as the legal system— but these institutions are less developed in international relations.

There is also less agreement about how to share power in these contexts.

Despite the limitations to Rawls's approach, *A Theory of Justice* creates many new ideas that are still helpful for thinking about politics. More than 40 years after the text was published, Rawls's work is repeatedly referred to in discussions on a whole range of issues: from human rights, democratization,* and toleration,* to development,* pluralism,* and constitutionalism* and democratization.*

Rawls's theory provoked an extensive debate when it was published. That debate is still ongoing. But even those who oppose his ideas applaud his work; the American philosopher Michael Sandel,* a critic of Rawls's thought, for example, says that *A Theory of Justice* is "deservedly celebrated."[7]

NOTES

1   Eric Gregory, "Before the Original Position: The Neo-Orthodox Theology of the Young John Rawls," *Journal of Religious Ethics* 35, no. 2 (2007): 195–6.

2   John Rawls, *A Theory of Justice* (Cambridge, MA: Belknap Press of Harvard University Press, 1999), 4.

3   Among Rawls's first important publications preceding his theory is his article "Justice as Fairness," *The Philosophical Review* 67, no. 2 (1958).

4   See Rawls, *A Theory of Justice*, 118–22.

5   Rawls, *A Theory of Justice*, 17–19.

6   Rawls, *A Theory of Justice*, 72.

7   Michael J. Sandel, *Liberalism and the Limits of Justice*, 2nd ed. (Cambridge: Cambridge University Press, 1998), ix.

SECTION 1
INFLUENCES

THE AUTHOR AND THE HISTORICAL CONTEXT

KEY POINTS

- John Rawls's seminal work *A Theory of Justice* is one of the most influential works of political philosophy* in the last 50 years.

- In childhood, Rawls was affected by the death of two of his brothers; his exposure to his mother's work on women's rights; and his friendships with children from poor or minority backgrounds.

- Rawls's experiences in World War II* precipitated his interest in the concept of justice.

Why Read This Text?

John Rawls's book *A Theory of Justice* was first published in 1971. It created a new school of political philosophy, Rawlsianism, and led to a flurry of scholarly thinking about justice and what this term means. Rawls's ideas and methodology sparked continuing discussions.

One reason Rawls's work is considered so important is that it offers an alternative to the philosophy of utilitarianism.* Utilitarianism looks at justice from the standpoint of society as a whole: its supporters argue that decisions should be made by considering which outcome would provide the greatest good for the greatest number of people. This approach looks at justice in the context of collective social benefit, but ignores the needs of the individual. In contrast, Rawls explores justice from the standpoint of the individual. For Rawls, justice requires that every person be treated "fairly": enjoying basic living standards and being given opportunities to move up in society.

> 66 I have often wondered why my religious beliefs changed, particularly during the war. I started out as a believing orthodox Episcopalian Christian, and abandoned it entirely by June of 1945 ... Three incidents stand out in my memory: Kilei Ridge,* Deacon's death, hearing and thinking about the Holocaust.* 99
>
> John Rawls, "On My Religion"

It is hard to find a work of political theory after 1971 that does not engage with his work. *A Theory of Justice* has been published in two editions and is available in over 20 languages. Rawls argues that his ideas can be applied universally, in any time and any place. The number of translations supports this argument, as scholars from many different states, political systems, and religious traditions continue to read and address his work.

Author's Life

Born in 1921 in the US city of Baltimore, Maryland, Rawls was from an upper-middle-class family. Both of his parents were practicing Christians and were active in politics. His father was a member of the Democratic Party and participated in local government and politics, and his mother was active in the local women's rights movement. But tragedy struck the family. As a child Rawls lost two younger brothers to illnesses—diphtheria and pneumonia—that they contracted from him. Sadly, these deaths occurred within a year of each other; they left Rawls with the lasting impression that life was both short and inherently unfair.[2]

Rawls attended faith-based schools, where he achieved excellent marks and as a young man he considered joining the priesthood and pursuing theological studies; he eventually decided to study philosophy and public ethics. After receiving his undergraduate degree from Princeton University, he joined the US Army in 1943 and fought in World War II, before returning to Princeton to complete his PhD. This was followed by a Fulbright Fellowship to Oxford University, where he met innovative thinkers such H. L. A. Hart,* an influential philosopher of law, the liberal* philosopher Isaiah Berlin,* and the political philosopher Stuart Hampshire.*[3] These scholars played a central role in the debates over political theory in the 1950s and were key influences for Rawls.[4]

His thinking was also shaped by world events of the time. At the end of World War II Rawls had been deployed in Japan. He was deeply affected by the nuclear bombardment of Hiroshima,* the first use of nuclear weapons in warfare, as well as by the Holocaust* (in the course of which the Nazis* murdered some 11 million European people, the greater part of whom were Jewish), and later by the ongoing American war in Vietnam,* which Rawls actively opposed.[5]

Author's Background

In 1971, when *A Theory of Justice* was first published, American society was experiencing rapid change; with this came violent clashes between its different social groups. Only a few years earlier the country had witnessed the flowering of the civil rights movement,* a social movement that successfully brought the suffering of America's racial minorities to the forefront of national consciousness. Internationally, the country was preoccupied with the Vietnam War. The conflict, in which the United States fought on behalf of South Vietnam against communist* North Vietnam, was the first to be broadcast on television; for the first time the American public was exposed to the violent reality of war. By the late 1960s, the conflict had divided society; many questioned the United States' ideas about justice and society's sense of fairness was shaken to the core—something evident in *A Theory of Justice.*

But what is also present is the awareness of what people can achieve when they work together towards a common goal. The 1960s, as well as being a decade of great upheaval, was also a time of great social achievements and idealism. In 1965, President Lyndon B. Johnson* signed the Civil Rights Act* into law. For the first time, all citizens were promised equal opportunities: people could vote, do business, and go to school without suffering racial discrimination. Four years later, in July 1969, the Apollo moon landings took place. The Americans were achieving things that had been thought impossible a decade earlier.

A Theory of Justice is of its time. Rawls questions fundamental assumptions about goodness and justice while believing that, through cooperation, it is possible to achieve them.

NOTES

1   Deacon was a friend of Rawls who also fought in World War II.

2   Thomas Winfried Pogge and Michelle Kosch, *John Rawls: His Life and Theory of Justice* (London: Oxford University Press, 2007), 5.

3   Pogge and Kosch, *John Rawls*, 16.

4   For example, Rawls refers to Hart when proposing a distinction between the concept of justice and the various conceptions of justice that may recur among different persons: John Rawls, *A Theory of Justice*, rev. ed. (Cambridge, MA: Belknap Press of Harvard University Press, 1999), 5. More generally, Hart's theory is used by Rawls to define several key concepts of its theory. Equally, Berlin is used as a reference for the concept of liberty and the debate regarding its definitions: Rawls, *A Theory of Justice*, 177.

5   Later he would publish an article in which he argued against the use of indiscriminate weapons against civilians in Hiroshima and Tokyo. See John Rawls, "50 Years After Hiroshima," *Dissent* (summer 1995): 323–7.

MODULE 2
ACADEMIC CONTEXT

KEY POINTS

- Political theory is concerned with the ideas that form the foundation of any society. Political theorists usually try to imagine how to create a society that helps people live the "good life."

- Major schools of political theory include utilitarianism,* which seeks the greatest good for the greatest number of people, liberalism,* which seeks the greatest good for individuals, and contractarianism,* according to which individual people make a contract with the state in exchange for state provision of the means to a "good life."

- Rawls works in the liberal and contractarian traditions.

The Work in its Context

When John Rawls published *A Theory of Justice* in 1971 the academic field of political theory was facing a severe challenge. International relations were then defined by the Cold War,* a long period of tension between the United States and the Soviet Union* and nations aligned to each, dividing the capitalist* world from the communist* world; across the world, states felt compelled to choose a side in this war of ideologies. Both camps believed that they knew the right way to order society. Both argued their case on the grounds of utilitarian philosophy, arguing that their system would achieve the best possible outcomes for the greatest number of people—although some people would, inevitably, not benefit.

But Rawls wanted a political theory that would create good social outcomes *without* harm to individuals. He makes this clear when he

> **❝** My aim is to present a conception of justice which generalizes and carries to a higher level of abstraction the familiar theory of the social contract as found, say, in Locke, Rousseau, and Kant. **❞**
>
> John Rawls, *A Theory of Justice*

says: "Just as each person must decide by rational reflection what constitutes his good … so a group of persons must decide once and for all what is to count among them as just and unjust."[1]

In order to find a path between the extremes of existing political ideas, Rawls turns to the idea of the social contract,* found in the works of thinkers like the English philosopher John Locke* and the Swiss-born philosopher Jean-Jacques Rousseau.* The social contract is an implicit agreement of cooperation between individuals in order to create a mutually beneficial society. But, in the tradition of the German philosopher Immanuel Kant,* Rawls adds a moral and ethical dimension to this. His starting point is the individual's rational desire to have a just and fair life within society.[2] In *A Theory of Justice* he devises a system that societies can use to decide what is just. Rawls argues that this system can be applied to any society at any time.

Overview of the Field

Rawls frequently refers to Kant, a deeply influential thinker notable for his ethical works such as *The Metaphysics of Morals* (1797). In it, Kant uses hypothetical situations to show how (rational) people can construct moral ideas that can be accepted throughout society. Rawls tends to agree with Kant that rational people are "autonomous moral agents"—that is, individuals free to think about good and bad in their own terms. Rawls also uses one of Kant's key methodologies: he puts his reader in an imagined situation and asks them—from that theoretical perspective—to describe what it means for a state to be just, fair and good.[3]

Rawls explicitly says that *A Theory of Justice* tries to offer an alternative to the utilitarian views of political theory. In the introduction to his book he argues that utilitarianism became popular largely because of the brilliance of the people who first proposed it. Rawls says that the British philosophers David Hume,* Adam Smith,* and Jeremy Bentham* were all "social theorists and economists of the first rank." But he also argues that their moral theories lacked clarity. There are many cases where it is hard to reconcile morality with a strict version of social utility.

For example: following Bentham, a state facing a lack of food or money might decide to let the weakest or least productive members of society die. That would help the state provide resources to people who can actively contribute to that society. But Rawls says that most people would rebel against the idea of sacrificing the old and the sick. Most societies give these groups special attention and consideration. Rawls's stated aim in *A Theory of Justice* is to create a "workable and systematic moral conception to oppose [utilitarianism]."[4]

Academic Influences

John Rawls is very open about the people and philosophies that influenced his work. His aims are to provide a definition of justice and, through that, to help people create just societies. These aims have been shared by thinkers throughout history. Indeed, Rawls writes that the "leading ideas are classical and well known." Locke, working in the seventeenth century, discusses the idea of a contract existing between individuals and the state. He argues that people enter into this contract with the understanding that the state will provide them with the ability to secure "life, liberty, and Estate."[5] Locke's thinking was complemented by the ideas of Rousseau, who views people as born free, but enslaved by society. Society, Rousseau argues, does not allow individuals to govern themselves or to have their own moral values.

Kant provides the last link in this chain. He argues that people should not be seen as the means to an end, but as an end in themselves—an idea he calls the categorical imperative.* For Kant, this approach provides a foundation from which people can think rationally about how they would wish to be treated by others. He is interested in how the dignity of each individual human being may be preserved.

These philosophers had a profound influence on Rawls's thought. But Rawls was also part of a vibrant intellectual community at both Oxford and Harvard and he mentions a number of his contemporaries who influenced his ideas. These individuals include well-known scholars like the Indian-born philosopher Amartya Sen,* the American philosopher Robert Nozick,* and the Latvian-born political theorist Judith Shklar.*[6] Although Nozick criticized Rawls's ideas, Rawls acknowledged that he found these criticisms useful. In contrast, Sen and Shklar both use some of Rawls's ideas in their own works.[7]

NOTES

1   John Rawls, *A Theory of Justice*, rev. ed. (Cambridge, MA: Belknap Press of Harvard University Press, 1999), 10–11.

2   Rawls, *A Theory of Justice*, 10–12. See also his earlier work on "Justice as Fairness," *The Philosophical Review* 67, no. 2 (1958): 164–94.

3   Rawls, *A Theory of Justice*, 10–11.

4   Rawls, *A Theory of Justice*, xviii.

5   John Locke, *Two Treatises of Government*, trans. Peter Laslett (Cambridge: Cambridge University Press, 1988), 323.

6   Rawls, *A Theory of Justice*, xxi.

7   See Amartya Sen, *On Economic Inequality* (Oxford: Oxford University Press, 1973); Robert Nozick, "Distributive Justice," *Philosophy & Public Affairs* (1973): 45–126; Judith Shklar, "Giving Injustice Its Due," *Yale Law Journal* (1989): 1135–51.

THE PROBLEM

KEY POINTS

- In *A Theory of Justice* John Rawls seeks to define justice and to provide society with tools that will help it to become more just.

- At the time when *A Theory of Justice* was being written, the most popular vision of justice was utilitarian:* justice, that is, was considered a question of achieving good outcomes for the greatest number of people.

- Seeking to create a theory of justice that could apply to any group of people at any time or place, Rawls rejected utilitarianism as it did not protect the rights of the individual.

Core Question

The central question asked by John Rawls in *A Theory of Justice* is: what principles should a just society be founded on? In the text Rawls justifies the importance of this question. Any society is based on shared ideas. What should be the foundation of these ideas? Rawls's answer is: truth. How can truth can be protected and embodied within social institutions? His answer is: through justice. This analogy between truth in philosophy and justice in social institutions is how Rawls justifies the central question of his inquiry. Justice (that upholds truth) is the fundamental social virtue of societies. It is, therefore, a legitimate object of inquiry for thinkers committed to making societies better.[1]

When Rawls was writing, utilitarian thought was dominant in the field of political philosophy.* Utilitarianism argues that justice is served when a system achieves a desired good for society as a whole. While this argument ignores individuals, it is equally true that

> **❝** Now as far as possible the basic structure should be appraised from the position of equal citizenship. This position is defined by the rights and liberties required by the principle of equal liberty and the principle of fair equality of opportunity. When the two principles are satisfied, all are equal citizens, and so everyone holds this position. **❞**
>
> John Rawls, *A Theory of Justice*

completely individualistic theories do not promote equality or fairness.

Rawls takes a novel approach to social contract* theory to solve this problem. He says that each person in a state is an equal citizen. Each person can think about what it means for a state to provide equal opportunity and fairness. This does not mean that Rawls advocates a communist* approach, which pursues equal outcomes for all people. Instead, he says that all citizens should have equal liberty (equal freedom under the law) and equality of opportunity. This means that although some people will achieve more than others, this will happen in a fair—that is, just—way.

The Participants

When Rawls wrote *A Theory of Justice*, most political theorists were using a utilitarian approach to justice (an approach founded on the assumption that any given political system should be judged on its ability to create good outcomes for as many people as possible). The English philosopher Jonathan Harrison* wrote, for example, that the universal duty to be just requires a universally applicable theory that can only be found in utilitarianism. Several other writers, among them the English economist R. F. Harrod,* were trying to revise classical utilitarianism to include modern social science, economics, and a more nuanced moral system. Similarly, the English philosopher Henry Sidgwick* sought to demonstrate that utilitarianism was a moral theory that could be applied to questions of economic and social justice.[2]

While most of these thinkers were aware that utilitarianism could be used to justify atrocities in the name of the common good, they saw it as the best way to create socially beneficial political systems nonetheless. Rather than trying to produce an alternative political theory, they tried to find ways of dealing with the moral dilemmas that utilitarianism created. A concern with morality had always been central to utilitarian thinkers. The British philosophers David Hume* and Jeremy Bentham,* the main proponents of this school of thought, explicitly mention morality in the titles of their works. Hume wrote *An Enquiry Concerning the Principles of Morals* (1751), while Bentham wrote *The Principles of Morals and Legislation* (1789).[3]

The Contemporary Debate

In *A Theory of Justice*, Rawls argues against utilitarian ideas and what he calls "intuitionism."* By this, he means that a society based on utilitarianism relies on human intuition to know when it is about to cross a moral or ethical boundary that should not be violated. Rawls says this view is "not irrational; and there is no assurance that we can do better. But this is no reason not to try."[4]

Rawls points out that intuitionism means that people rely on their principles to ascertain whether a boundary is about to be violated. But intuitionism does not provide any method or rules to decide which principles are the most important. This means that it is quite easy for people to hold conflicting principles, making it impossible to create a rational (or a universal) morality. Rawls specifically mentions the American philosopher Robert Nozick's* critiques. In his "Moral Complications and Moral Structures," Nozick points out that people can come to very different conclusions about what is "self-evident" or a "necessary moral principle."[5]

But Rawls does not simply critique utilitarian or intuitionist ideas. In *A Theory of Justice* he offers an alternative way of thinking. To determine the justness of a particular system, he proposes two key principles:

- The rules that define basic freedoms should "apply to everyone equally." People should have the most liberty possible that does not interfere with other people's liberties.
- Where the system allows for inequalities, it should do so only in order to benefit each person.[6] As an example, if someone is incentivized to carry out socially useful work that benefits other people, all individuals may agree that they are better off if that inequality exists.

While Rawls's ideas are grounded in traditional social contract theory (the liberal* idea that it is worth forgoing certain liberties if the state can guarantee security and political rights), they also offer a new and alternative approach to political theory.

NOTES

1 John Rawls, *A Theory of Justice*, rev. ed. (Cambridge, MA: Belknap Press of Harvard University Press, 1999), 3.

2 See Rawls, *A Theory of Justice*, 20 cf.

3 Rawls, *A Theory of Justice*, 20 cf.

4 Rawls, *A Theory of Justice*, xviii.

5 Rawls, *A Theory of Justice*, 30.

6 Rawls, *A Theory of Justice*, 56.

THE AUTHOR'S CONTRIBUTION

KEY POINTS

- Rawls's primary aim in *A Theory of Justice* is to create a new and rational way for people to build a just and fair society. He wants to provide alternatives to theories such as Marxism* (the analysis and philosophy derived from the thought of the German economist and political philosopher* Karl Marx)* and utilitarianism.*

- Rawls shows how he arrives at his conclusions, allowing the reader to understand how he has formed his view of justice.

- Rawls does not require people to accept his definition of justice. He simply provides a system to help societies define what they understand by it.

Author's Aims

John Rawls's book *A Theory of Justice* is written in the tradition of liberal* political theory. Rawls proposes a theory of justice that sees the individual as a moral rational agent—capable of acting morally according to rational thought—and defends the principle of absolute freedom. His work epitomizes the idea that there can be a universal concept of human rights.* For Rawls these rights take precedence over the different ethical positions that can be found within a pluralist*society (that is, a society that permits difference, notably in political belief).

These liberal, pluralist values underlie Rawls's two key principles:

- The principle of equal freedom, according to which "each person is to have an equal right to the most extensive scheme of equal basic liberties compatible with a similar scheme of liberties for

> 66 I have tried to present the theory of justice as a viable systematic doctrine so that the idea of maximizing the good does not hold sway by default. The criticism of teleological* theories cannot fruitfully proceed piecemeal. We must attempt to construct another kind of view which has the same virtues of clarity and system but which yields a more discriminating interpretation of our moral sensibilities. 99
>
> John Rawls, *A Theory of Justice*

others."[1] In other words, individuals should have freedom of action, as long as their freedom does not detract from the freedom of others.

- The principle of difference,* according to which an unequal distribution of goods in a just society can be tolerated only as far as this distribution is beneficial to the least advantaged persons of that society. Furthermore, these inequalities must be attached to offices and positions that are open to all.

Rawls acknowledges that he is indebted to the tradition of liberal thinking epitomized by the German philosopher Immanuel Kant.[*2] His theories overlap with the social contract* ideas of both Kant and the Swiss-born philosopher Jean-Jacques Rousseau.[*3] However, Rawls's ideas are also groundbreaking. Unlike Kant, Rawls claims that his principles of justice are not abstract, but are rooted in analysis and can be reproduced. Rawls also approaches the concept of the social contract in a new way. He uses it as a tool to help people think about the legitimacy of the way a given society is structured. In essence, Rawls claims his philosophical approach is closer to a science than an art.

Approach

Rawls explains his goals. He discusses other ways of conceptualizing a just society and explains his objections to them. Then, carefully and methodically, he defines a number of concepts and tools—"thought experiments"*—that help the reader to follow his reasoning and test his ideas. Rawls's hypothesis is that his ideas about justice can be universally applied: they can be accepted as rational in any society at any time.

The concepts Rawls creates include: the "original position,"*[4] the "veil of ignorance,"* and "reflective equilibrium."*

According to the "original position," if a rational person had a blank canvas to create a new society, what would they want that society to achieve? How could they best create a society that meets these goals?

With the "veil of ignorance," Rawls offers us the opportunity to consider what a fair society would mean to the least advantaged member of that society. He challenges his readers to think about creating a society from a position of ignorance about their own place in that society. The veil of ignorance assumes "no one knows his place in society, his class position or social status, nor does any one know his fortune in the distribution of natural assets and abilities, his intelligence, strength, and the like."[5]

"Reflective equilibrium," finally, asks readers to reevaluate their preexisting principles by going back and forth to examine their ideas until they reach a point of equilibrium.[6]

These philosophical exercises help people define justice. Rawls challenges the idea that history has a "given end": a supposition found in many philosophies, such as the absolute equality in material things envisioned by Marxism. He also challenges the orthodoxy of liberalism and social contract theory, which says that justice is restricted by fundamental truths about human nature. Rawls argues that justice can be created through human reflection.

Contribution in Context

Rawls is not the first political theorist to discuss the concept of justice. Neither is he the first to define justice in terms of what is good for the individual within society. He built upon the thinking of writers like John Locke,* the influential English political philosopher who argued that governments rule by the consent of the governed. Locke argues that individuals do this to gain security for their natural rights: life, liberty, and property. The social contract tradition implies that a government that does not secure these natural rights is illegitimate. But Rawls goes further. He claims that people are naturally equal, and we can prove that all people should be treated as equal citizens by imagining ourselves behind the veil of ignorance in the original position.

Rawls's approach combines the social contract tradition, with the notion, following Kant, that the individual person is the primary unit that people should consider in these questions. In a theological tradition the self-centeredness of people is a weakness. For Rawls, it is an aspect of humanity that can be used to make people think *less* selfishly. By imagining they might be at the bottom of a given society, people will try to create a society that is fair to all its members.

In this combination of the selfish and the social, the practical and the moral, Rawls is a highly unique thinker. He draws upon Locke and Kant for inspiration, and Jeremy Bentham* and David Hume* for contrast, to create his own novel system for thinking rationally about justice.

NOTES

1   John Rawls, *A Theory of Justice*, rev. ed. (Cambridge, MA: Belknap Press of Harvard University Press, 1999), 53.

2   Rawls, *A Theory of Justice*, 221–7.

3   Rawls, *A Theory of Justice*, 10.

4   Rawls, *A Theory of Justice*, 118–22.

5   Rawls, *A Theory of Justice*, 10–11.

6   Rawls, *A Theory of Justice*, 17–19.

SECTION 2
IDEAS

MAIN IDEAS

KEY POINTS

- Rawls examines the theory of justice; the institutions of just societies and governments; and the ends—the desired outcomes—of a just society.

- Rawls's main argument is that people can rationally derive principles for justice by defining an acceptably fair society for the least well-off.

- Rawls aims to use a philosophical and scientific approach to the question of justice; his goal is to make his work rational and universally applicable.

Key Themes

In *A Theory of Justice* John Rawls famously defined justice as "fairness." He conceived a just society as one that had equal citizenship and equal opportunity at its heart. To explore those ideas he used an approach he called "reflective equilibrium":*[1] he outlines a particular political problem or debate, examines opinions about that topic, analyzes their strengths and weaknesses, then adjusts his own ideas in light of those strengths and weaknesses. This process makes his own theory more balanced and solid. He divides his work into three parts: the theory of justice; the institutions of just societies and governments; and the ends (the desired outcomes) of a just society.

Rawls's work is motivated by his dissatisfaction with utilitarian* political theory. He argues that despite the utilitarian claim to morality this philosophy can lead to deeply amoral policy since it does not offer people a way to prioritize different virtues, or even a way to decide what virtues their society could pursue. He also points out that

> ❝ First: each person is to have an equal right to the most extensive scheme of basic liberties compatible with a similar scheme of liberties for others.
>
> Second: social and economic inequalities are to be arranged so that they are both (a) reasonably expected to be to everyone's advantage, and (b) attached to positions and offices open to all. ❞
>
> John Rawls, *A Theory of Justice*

utilitarianism offers no mechanism by which consensus can be reached about what is most beneficial to society.

The subjectivity of intuitionism* (the process, roughly, of arriving at a solution to some philosophical problem by using intuition to weigh each side of the argument) means it cannot be used legitimately to translate ethical reasoning into social policy. Rawls outlines the weaknesses of utilitarianism and offers his own alternative: an argument that freedom must be as broad as possible, limited only when one individual's freedom of action interferes with someone else's freedoms.

Exploring the Ideas

Rawls starts his book by outlining the evolution of utilitarian and intuitionist ideas over the course of the period of European intellectual history known as the Enlightenment* (roughly, mid-1600s to early 1800s) and into the Industrial Age* (the period, which began in the mid-eighteenth century, when we moved from societies founded on agriculture to societies founded on industry).

He argues that to create a fair society, people need to imagine what kind of society they would create *if they had no idea what their role in that society would be*. He calls this the "original position."* This requires an imaginary ignorance he calls "the veil of ignorance."* It is a demanding process; it is difficult to assume that one could be at the absolute bottom of society. It is as though Rawls asks his readers to wear a blindfold, clear their minds, and then orient themselves in a completely imagined society.[2]

Rawls argues that, through doing this, two key principles of a just society become self-evident: that all people must be equal citizens before the law, and that social differences and inequalities are acceptable only if they create more desirable outcomes for the whole society; to be acceptable it must also be the case that anyone could potentially hold the higher status or the better-paid jobs.[3] This is often called the "difference principle."*

Rawls compares the assumptions and outcomes of his approach with those of utilitarianism.

While Part One of Rawls's text is inherently philosophical, Part Two is distinctly political. Here, Rawls defines liberty and discusses its limitations, his ideas closely mirroring those of the philosopher John Locke.*[4] However, where Rawls innovates is in combining these ideas with ethics following the thought of Immanuel Kant.* These give his work a moral overtone: for Rawls, equating justice with fairness and personal freedom is not only the reasonable thing to do, it is the *right* thing to do. This part of the text looks at issues such as economics, the distribution of goods, and social duties. Rawls addresses issues including civil disobedience (a form of protest in which certain laws are deliberately disobeyed) and conscientious refusal (the decision not to serve in the military as a matter of conscience) which reflect the influence of events like the American civil rights movement* and the Vietnam War.*

In Part Three, Rawls offers a method for thinking about morality based on rational, agnostic, deduction rather than religious thought. Critics could, however, argue that his moral reasoning is not objective, but simply reflects Rawls's own subjective moral preferences. Rawls himself addresses the ideas of psychology* and the human desire to find meaning.[5]

Language and Expression

A Theory of Justice is a very demanding text. Rawls's audience was fellow philosophers and academics. He assumes that his readers are familiar with key political theories and already know the most important thinkers in these traditions. He moves frequently between philosophy, analogy, and discussions of historical philosophy, while introducing complicated ways to define complex concepts. This text was developed over many years and takes criticism of his earlier work into account.

Rawls's most crucial argument, his definition of "justice as fairness,"* dates back to 1958. This was the year when he first introduced the term, using it as the title of an article in *The Philosophical Review*. Much of his work originated in papers written for academic journals and the book reflects that. It uses specialist terms, it has a complicated structure, and it makes frequent use of footnotes to offer textual evidence or further explanation. This rigorous approach gained his ideas notice and credibility within academia. Rawls's book was so thorough that even those who fundamentally disagreed with it felt compelled to explain their disagreement.

In this sense, the book can be judged to be highly influential. In fact, it has been so successful that Rawls is one of the few political theorists whose ideas are (occasionally) acknowledged by politicians and government officials.

NOTES

1   John Rawls, *A Theory of Justice*, rev. ed. (Cambridge, MA: Belknap Press of Harvard University Press, 1999), 17–19.

2   Rawls, *A Theory of Justice*, 15–18.

3   Rawls, *A Theory of Justice*, 52–64.

4   See John Locke, *Locke on Toleration*, ed. Richard Vernon (Cambridge: Cambridge University Press, 2010), for his views on how much toleration and freedom are proper in society.

5   Rawls, *A Theory of Justice*, 429–33.

MODULE 6
SECONDARY IDEAS

KEY POINTS

- Key amongst the secondary ideas in Rawls's work is the concept of the "original position":* the blank canvas upon which a just society can be created.
- Several scholars have studied Rawls's tools and concepts, believing them to be valuable in their own right.
- While Part Three of *A Theory of Justice* has been overlooked, there is growing academic interest in this section of Rawls's work.

Other Ideas

One of the most important secondary ideas in John Rawls's *A Theory of Justice* is the thought experiment* he calls the "original position"— an imaginative exercise he uses to draw conclusions about the nature of justice and its relationship to the state. Rawls uses a number of techniques to help his reader step outside his or her awareness of their own societal position, allowing them to consider how true justice would look to people no matter what position they occupy within society. He calls this lack of awareness of status (of wealth, profession, abilities, intellect, or even individual moral preferences) the "veil of ignorance,"* arguing that thinkers adopting the original position can achieve consensus on the nature of justice. This is because the original position "excludes the knowledge of those contingencies which set men at odds and allow them to be guided by their prejudices."[1]

Another key idea in the text is the concept of "reflective equilibrium":* going back to ideas, reflecting on their strengths and weaknesses, and adjusting these ideas to take account of those strengths

> ❝ We may define self-respect (or self-esteem) as having two aspects. First of all, as we noted earlier, it includes a person's sense of his own value, his secure conviction that his conception of his good, his plan of life, is worth carrying out. And second, self-respect implies a confidence in one's ability, so far as it is within one's power, to fulfill one's intentions. ❞
>
> John Rawls, *A Theory of Justice*

and weaknesses. Although this concept is not discussed at great length in the text, its influence pervades every argument Rawls makes. While *A Theory of Justice* is a long and in some ways repetitive book, the repetition occurs as a result of Rawls refining his ideas in order to reach a point of reflective equilibrium (achieved at roughly 500 pages of discussion).

It is difficult to speak of Rawls's secondary ideas in isolation. They are closely interwoven and Rawls uses them as tools to show the readers how his thought has developed. In other words, his secondary ideas give shape to the content of his thought on justice and fairness.

Exploring the Ideas

Rawls believes that his concept of the original position is vital for helping people come to rational, universal conclusions about social justice. He emphasizes that the original position is a hypothetical construct. It is an idea, however, that has been criticized for being impossible to imagine. Rawls replies that "the hypothetical nature of the original position invites the question: why should we take any interest in it, moral or otherwise? Recall the answer: the conditions embodied in the description of this situation are ones that we do in fact accept. Or if we do not, then we can be persuaded to do so by philosophical considerations of the sort occasionally introduced."[2]

This statement is remarkably confident. Rawls has thought about justice for many years. His approach is careful and methodical. As a result, he makes the (very large) assumption that other people who reflect on these issues equally carefully will draw the same conclusions.

Why bother, then, with the thought experiment of the original position? Because we already accept its premises, and even if we do not, Rawls can convince us that they are correct.

It is ironic that one of the political ideologies Rawls most stridently rejects, Marxism,* makes a similar assumption: that those who reject it are simply being influenced by "false consciousness." Once properly educated about the truth of their social and political situation, the supposition is that they will inevitably agree with Marx.* In this sense, Rawls's theory runs the danger of becoming an ideology proper: a view of the world that is certain of its assumptions and assertive in its prescriptions.

Overlooked

Part Three of *A Theory of* Justice is one of the most neglected sections of Rawls's text.[3] Rawls discusses justice in relation to moral psychology* and introduces the idea of a "sentiment of justice"—the idea that the individuals who make up a given society share a common view of justice. Following this discussion, Rawls looks at the outcome for a society that shares a common understanding of justice. He argues that when a society's ideas about justice align with their social values the society can be called well ordered. A well-ordered society is likely to enjoy stability. Rawls also claims that when a people share a common sentiment of justice, it helps society remain committed to justice as a common good.

It is only recently that scholars have shown revived interest in this part of Rawls's theory. One relevant example is the work of the American philosopher Paul Weithman.*[4] His work addresses Rawls's shift from his original theory of justice to subsequent work in which he discusses political liberalism.*[5] Weithman argues that *A Theory of Justice* is not as individualist and Kantian—founded on the ideas of Immanuel Kant*—as many other scholars have believed. He uses Rawls's ideas about stability and the sentiment of justice to suggest that Rawls's philosophy relies on a "sense of justice."[6] This refers to people's capacity to develop a shared morality upon which the stability of a well-ordered society is based.

NOTES

1   John Rawls, *A Theory of Justice*, rev. ed. (Cambridge, MA: Belknap Press of Harvard University Press, 1999), 15–17.

2   Rawls, *Theory of Justice*, 514.

3   Rawls, *Theory of Justice*, 347–514.

4   Paul J. Weithman, *Why Political Liberalism? On John Rawls's Political Turn* (New York and Oxford: Oxford University Press, 2011).

5   Particularly in the collected essays in John Rawls, *Political Liberalism* (New York: Columbia University Press, 1993).

6   According to Rawls, "A sense of justice is an effective desire to apply and act from the principles of justice and so from the point of view of justice." Rawls, *A Theory of Justice*, 497.

MODULE 7
ACHIEVEMENT

KEY POINTS

- Rawls wanted to convince others that his approach to justice was reasonable, rational, and achievable (at least in theory).

- The painstaking explanation of his ideas, his tools for thinking about the ideal society, and the quality of his philosophical arguments all demanded serious attention.

- While Rawls influenced the debate on justice and became one of the most important thinkers in this area, he was limited by his reliance on the liberal* tradition and its universalist assumptions (that is, its assumptions that its arguments are applicable in all circumstances).

Assessing the Argument

In *A Theory of Justice* John Rawls assumes that his theory is applicable within well-ordered societies—but it may be that not all societies in the world reflect Rawls's criteria of "well ordered."[1]

One example would be a society that is hierarchical and characterized by an overarching ethical conception that informs its structure (as an example, a monarchy in which there are social inequalities that do not arise from the merits and capabilities of its citizens). Yet this society could still guarantee a decent level of basic rights to its members.[2] Rawls discusses this possibility in his later book *The Law of Peoples*. He uses an imaginary example: the state of Kazanistan. Rawls argues that liberals should not intervene in the affairs of this society, since this would be in breach of the liberal principle of tolerance. This example represents a limitation to the ideas that Rawls's theories have universal validity.

> 66 Without denying that actual political achievement of the ideal is important, he [Rawls] believed that a well-grounded belief in its achievability can reconcile us to the world. So long as we are justifiably confident that a self-sustaining and just collective life among human beings is realistically possible, we may hope that we or others will someday, somewhere, achieve it – and can then also work towards this achievement … political philosophy can provide an inspiration that can banish the dangers of resignation and cynicism and can enhance the value of our lives even today. 99
>
> Thomas Pogge, *John Rawls: His Life and Theory of Justice*

Scholars such as the American political theorist Charles Beitz* and the German philosopher Thomas Pogge* have argued (in different ways) that Rawls's theory regarding equal liberty and the principle of difference* can be applied universally; in contrast to Rawls himself, Beitz and Pogge argue that the cultural differences between nations do not necessarily represent a limitation on the possibility of recognizing universal human rights,* such as social and economic rights, and global social justice. In *The Law of Peoples*, Rawls argues that only fundamental human rights are universal.

Achievement in Context

Even those who disagree with Rawls praise his work. One of his sharpest critics, the Canadian-born Marxist* philosopher Gerald Cohen,* writes that "at most two books in the history of Western political philosophy* have a claim to be regarded as greater than *A Theory of Justice*: Plato's* *Republic* and Hobbes's* *Leviathan*."[3] As soon as *A Theory of Justice* was published it was considered an essential text.

Rawls's ideas pulled the focus of political theory away from the utilitarian* notion of the "common good" and toward the good of the individual.

Rawls was writing in the midst of the Cold War*—a long period of military and diplomatic tensions characterized, in part, by its competing ideologies of democracy (the "Western Bloc" of the United States and its allies) and communism* (the "Eastern Bloc" of the Soviet Union* and the nations aligned to it). He sought to free political theory from its reliance on utilitarian moral philosophy and intuitionist* method (according to which intuition is a useful tool in the process of solving philosophical problems by weighing alternative solutions).

Instead, his aim was to create a liberal, contractarian* understanding of justice: an understanding, based on liberty and the idea that we agree on the condition of social life by contractually agreeing to certain obligations, that could be universally agreed on and achieved.[4]

While he succeeded in his desire to move political theory away from utilitarianism, the hope that his ideas offered a universal blueprint for creating justice, however, has been thoroughly tested by subsequent developments in global politics. Universality is not always the aim of a political theory, nor does every society wish to achieve a universally applicable model of government. The Cold War may have obscured that fact. The Soviet Union and the United States both sought to convince the world that their system was the best way to order society. Both nations believed they should give the gift of their civilizations to the world. Although Rawls rejects the belief in a predefined end of history that Marxism and liberalism can both display, he nonetheless reverts to similar universalist tendencies. Having spent two decades thinking about justice, Rawls asserts that his conclusions are those that any rational person would come to.

Despite this limitation, *A Theory of Justice* arguably became the most influential work of political theory of the late twentieth century.

It continues to be influential, indeed central, in the work of prominent thinkers like the Nobel Prize-winning philosopher and economist Amartya Sen.*[5]

Limitations

Rawls reflected on the controversial issue of whether or not his work applied universally in his later work. In his book *The Law of Peoples,*[6] he presents his thinking on international justice. Other scholars have also debated whether his theory can be globally applied and whether it works for societies that are not traditionally liberal.[7]

In *A Theory of Justice* Rawls discusses applying his ideas on an international scale. He claims that his thought experiment* of the "original position"* would only justify the first principle of justice: the right of each nation to be equally free. In this sense, Rawls's theory is universal. It justifies the ideas that nations should be equally free to exercise self-determination and self-defense.[8]

Rawls said that his second principle of justice—about distribution of opportunity—does not apply universally since it is based on a community that shares a common sense of justice. Even regions like the European Union, a body supposedly based on shared European values and identity, have faced considerable challenges in this area. It is hard to create a just system of apportioning funding and deciding on appropriate government spending policies. This limits, and perhaps even refutes, Rawls's theory of universal principles of justice.

It is, perhaps, the case that these principles apply only within the domestic context of a liberal society—one in which all members share a similar sense of justice.[9]

NOTES

1   For an introductory discussion of the concept of "well-ordered society," see Thomas Pogge and Michelle Kosch, *John Rawls: His Life and Theory of Justice* (Oxford and New York: Oxford University Press, 2007), 137–9.

2   See John Rawls, *The Law of Peoples: With "The Idea of Public Reason Revisited"* (Cambridge, MA: Harvard University Press, 1999).

3   G. A. Cohen, *Rescuing Justice and Equality* (Cambridge, MA: Harvard University Press, 2008), 11.

4   John Rawls, *A Theory of Justice*, rev. ed. (Cambridge, MA: Belknap Press of Harvard University Press, 1999), 10.

5   See Amartya Sen, *The Idea of Justice* (Cambridge, MA: Belknap Press of Harvard University Press, 2009).

6   Rawls, *Law of Peoples*.

7   Thomas Nagel, "The Problem of Global Justice," *Philosophy & Public Affairs* 33, no. 2 (2005): 113–47; Thomas Pogge, *World Poverty and Human Rights: Cosmopolitan Responsibilities and Reforms*, 2nd ed. (Cambridge: Polity, 2008); Charles R. Beitz, *Political Theory and International Relations*, 2nd ed. (Princeton, N.J.: Princeton University Press, 1999); Alasdair MacIntyre, *Whose Justice? Which Rationality?* (London: Duckworth, 1988).

8   Rawls, *A Theory of Justice*, 331–2.

9   Rawls, *A Theory of Justice*, 497.

PLACE IN THE AUTHOR'S WORK

KEY POINTS

- *A Theory of Justice* is the distillation of Rawls's work as an academic.

- In the book Rawls develops his earlier ideas about social justice, going beyond simple exploration of a concept to develop an entire system for understanding justice.

- *A Theory of Justice* made Rawls's name famous within the field of political philosophy;* he spent the rest of his career refining his arguments and responding to his many admirers and critics.

Positioning

By the time John Rawls published *A Theory of Justice* in 1971, he had already studied and worked at some of the world's most elite universities, including Oxford and Harvard. This was, however, his first publication in book form and it became the most relevant and acclaimed text he published. Parts of the work are derived from Rawls's previous papers and academic articles. He began work on the book itself in 1962. After several revisions, it was eventually published in 1971. By then Rawls was 50 years old and the chairman of the philosophy department at Harvard.

A Theory of Justice is a compilation and expansion of Rawls's earlier work. The issue of justice is central in nearly all of his texts. Rawls's biographer, the German–born philosopher Thomas Pogge,* notes that Rawls's lifelong study of justice was initially derived from his Christian religious ethos. It then became even more potent after he left his faith. Rawls needed to find a suitable alternative to religion on which to

> 66 Despite many criticisms of the original work, I
> still accept its main outlines and defend its central
> doctrines. Of course, I wish, as one might expect, that
> I had done certain things differently, and I would
> now make a number of important revisions. But if I
> were writing A Theory of Justice over again, I would
> not write, as authors sometimes say, a completely
> different book. 99
>
> John Rawls, preface to the revised edition, *A Theory of Justice*

ground his social ethics.[1] The third section of the book can be seen as
a reflection of Rawls's own social involvement. Outside academia he
was a member of various social justice movements and opposed the
Vietnam War.*

In 1999 Rawls published a second edition of *A Theory of Justice*.
Although he did not abandon or even significantly change any of his
main ideas or philosophical arguments in this edition, in the preface
he acknowledges a number of criticisms that he deemed especially
important or valid. He then directs the reader's attention to his
subsequent revisions. Rawls can be seen as a scholar who was seeking
to refine—rather than to reinvent or discard—his earlier ideas. Even
his revisions are in keeping with his belief in "reflective equilibrium":*
nearly all of them are to do with making his definitions and ideas
clearer and more precise.[2]

Integration

Rawls's body of work is extremely coherent. His entire body of work
can be viewed as a discussion of a few key themes: social justice,
fairness, human rights,* social ethics. These themes are discussed
repeatedly, as Rawls engages in a process of making them more

philosophically coherent, more politically relevant, and, he hoped, more persuasive.

We may consider *A Theory of Justice* to fundamentally describe Rawls's thought. In his subsequent publications, he is engaged in two main tasks. The first is that of clarifying, restating, or revising aspects of his theory by responding to his critics (his second book publication, the collection of essays entitled *Political Liberalism*,[3] was dedicated to this, as was the revised edition of *A Theory of Justice* published in 1999).

The second of Rawls's tasks was to develop and expand certain aspects of his theory. While *A Theory of Justice* is concerned mainly with domestic justice, Rawls's final publication, *The Law of Peoples*,[4] discusses justice in political theory with reference to the international political context. Here Rawls elaborates on the theory of international justice, which is briefly sketched in *A Theory of Justice*.[5] He developed these ideas further in a public lecture given for the human rights organization Amnesty International.*[6] Rawls sought to assess how far his ideas can be applied to the problems of international relations.

Significance

Rawls's boy of literary work is compact, consistent, and strictly focused on the subject of his academic research: studying the theory of a just society. In methodological and conceptual terms, Rawls's academic production remains consistent, even if subject to revisions and changes. The highly specialized vocabulary that Rawls defines in *A Theory of Justice* was to inform the entire political-theory debate in subsequent decades and remained substantially unaltered across various publications.

Although *A Theory of Justice* has provoked a number of critiques and refutations, its influence is unquestionable. Rawls shaped the scholarly debate about political theory and his intellectual and academic achievements could scarcely have been of higher quality or greater import.

Rawls's work was so influential that he was awarded the National Humanities Medal by President Bill Clinton* in 1999—a medal awarded for work that deepens the nation's understanding of the humanities. During a brief speech explaining the reasons John Rawls was being honored, President Clinton noted the impact his work had on him and his political development, as well as on his wife, Hillary. Clinton said that "when Hillary and I were in law school, we were among the millions" moved by Rawls's book. Rawls, Clinton said, "helped a whole generation of learned Americans revive their faith in democracy itself."[7]

NOTES

1   See John Rawls, "50 Years After Hiroshima," *Dissent* (summer 1995): 323–7. Also, Thomas Pogge and Michelle Kosch, *John Rawls: His Life and Theory of Justice* (Oxford and New York: Oxford University Press, 2007), 18–19.

2   John Rawls, *A Theory of Justice*, rev. ed. (Cambridge, MA: Belknap Press of Harvard University Press, 1999), xi–xvi.

3   John Rawls, *Political Liberalism* (New York: Columbia University Press, 1993).

4   John Rawls, *The Law of Peoples: With "The Idea of Public Reason Revisited"* (Cambridge, MA: Harvard University Press, 1999).

5   Rawls refers to the idea of the law of nations, which subsequently became the law of peoples, in paragraph 58 of *A Theory of Justice*, 331–5.

6   The lecture was then published as a paper in John Rawls, *Collected Papers*, ed. Samuel Richard Freeman (Cambridge, MA: Harvard University Press, 1999).

7   William J. Clinton, in *Public Papers of Presidents of the United States*: *William J. Clinton* (1999), 1628–9.

SECTION 3
IMPACT

THE FIRST RESPONSES

KEY POINTS

- Rawls is criticized by a number of thinkers on both the left and right of the political spectrum, especially on the issue of equality.

- Rawls admits that the issue of equality is the weakest link in his chain of reasoning.

- The ideas expressed in *A Theory of Justice* are so compelling that they sharpen the arguments of everyone involved in the debate, including thinkers who criticize Rawls's assumptions or goals.

Criticism

Only a few years after the publication of John Rawls's *A Theory of Justice* in 1971, the American philosopher Robert Nozick* published work arguing against Rawls's ideas of making society more equal through taxation and redistribution.[1] More criticism emerged from communitarian* thinkers. Communitarians reject the idea that humans can develop moral concepts independently of the society and community to which they belong.

Communitarian thinkers such as the Scottish philosopher Alasdair MacIntyre* and the Canadian philosopher Charles Taylor* were critical of the substance of Rawls's theory. They criticize the idea that humans were capable of moral impartiality and argue that the way Rawls prioritizes "the right" over "the good" is problematic.[2] MacIntyre argues that an individual's ethical ideas cannot be understood as disembodied from the cultural and historical tradition to which they belong—meaning that the idea that there is a universal,

> ❝ One of the most serious weaknesses was in the account of liberty, the defects of which were pointed out by H. L. A. Hart in his critical discussion of 1973 ... A second serious weakness of the original edition was its account of primary goods ... The revisions are too many to note here, but they do not, I think, depart in any important way from the view of the original edition. ❞
>
> John Rawls, preface to the revised edition, *A Theory of Justice*

human agreement on what is "right" is ahistorical and misleading.[3] Similarly, Taylor says it is impossible to abstract moral principles from the "social matrix" in which they are developed; in other words, what is right for a society cannot be separated from what is good for a person.[4] Another communitarian critic of Rawl, the American philosopher Michael Sandel,* challenges Rawls's idea of the original position.*[5] Sandel argues that it is impossible for an individual to be capable of abstract moral reason outside a given social and moral context.

Scholars on the left also criticize Rawls. The Marxist* scholar Gerald Cohen* argues that Rawls's version of equality is not egalitarian enough. According to Cohen, a truly egalitarian theory of justice cannot justify the degree of inequality that the Rawlsian principle of difference* concedes. He rejects Rawls's idea that inequality should be tolerated if it can be seen to benefit the least advantaged members of a society.[6]

Responses

Rawls addressed his critics in a number of different lectures and publications, and in a revised edition of *A Theory of Justice* (1999). His response to criticism was to incorporate any criticism that could weaken his theory into his argument, reflect on it, and adjust his ideas where he felt the criticism was valid. He also proposed counterarguments to his critics, which stimulated further academic debate.

In the revised edition of *A Theory of Justice*, Rawls addresses early criticism of his ideas from the British philosopher H. L. A. Hart.* Hart pointed out problems with Rawls's concept of liberty.[7] In response Rawls proposes revisions to his account of liberty. In others papers and lectures, Rawls answers his communitarian critics.[8] In his collection of essays *Political Liberalism*, Rawls points out that his theory is in fact a theory of *political* liberalism.* This means that he is discussing ethics in the context of the political sphere. This does not interfere with other ethical conceptions, as long as these are reasonable and do not violate the principles of justice. Political liberalism is not an overarching moral conception (unlike a religion); instead, it takes into account pluralism*—a political system that can accommodate people from a number of different backgrounds, notably in terms of ethnicity or religion.

Having clarified these points, Rawls adheres to the substance of his theory; he does not alter his ideas about justice within societies.

Conflict and Consensus

As we have seen, much important criticism came from communitarian thinkers. Particularly influential were arguments made by the philosophers Michael Sandel and Charles Taylor that individuals have comprehensive conceptions of the good and that these concepts inform our idea of justice and what is right. This counters Rawls's idea that what is *right* would, in a just society, take precedence over what is *good*.

Perhaps the most important development in Rawls's theory came with the publication of his book *The Law of Peoples*. This uses his fundamental theory of justice as a basis to discuss the issue of justice on an international scale.[9] In this book Rawls develops and significantly modifies the idea about international justice that he had briefly presented in *A Theory of Justice*. These modifications cannot, however, be primarily accredited to criticism from other scholars. They were due to Rawls's own awareness of the limits of his theory in the international political context.

The general perception amongst scholars is that no critique of Rawls's theory dealt a fatal blow to his work. Rawls's theory remains among the most accomplished examples of scholarship in the field of political theory. Critics of Rawls are still active, and indeed still critical—but his work remains a key reference in contemporary political theory, provoking original thought and debate.

NOTES

1   See, for example, Robert Nozick, *Anarchy, State, and Utopia* (Oxford: Blackwell, 1974). On the basis of the same theory, other political conceptions, such as the minimal state and anarchism, have been defended as ways of minimizing interference in people's negative freedom.

2   See Alasdair C. MacIntyre, *After Virtue: A Study in Moral Theory*, 3rd ed. (Notre Dame, IN: University of Notre Dame Press, 2007); and Charles Taylor, *Human Agency and Language: Philosophical Papers 1* (Cambridge: Cambridge University Press, 1985).

3   MacIntyre, *After Virtue*.

4   Taylor, *Human Agency and Language*.

5   Michael J. Sandel, *Liberalism and the Limits of Justice*, 2nd ed. (Cambridge: Cambridge University Press, 1998).

6   G. A. Cohen, *Rescuing Justice and Equality* (Cambridge, MA: Harvard University Press, 2008).

7   H. L. A. Hart, "Rawls on Liberty and Its Priority," *University of Chicago Law Review* 40, no. 3 (1973): 534–55.

8   John Rawls, *Political Liberalism* (New York: Columbia University Press, 1993).

9   John Rawls, *The Law of Peoples: With "The Idea of Public Reason Revisited"* (Cambridge, MA: Harvard University Press, 1999).

MODULE 10
THE EVOLVING DEBATE

KEY POINTS

- Supporters of Rawls have extended his thought into the sphere of international relations and global justice.

- Scholars sometimes self-identify as "Rawlsian" in order to express their general agreement with Rawls's ideas.

- *A Theory of Justice* continues to influence current political debates; Rawlsian ideas have been used, for example, to discuss economic and environmental issues.

Uses and Problems

Rawls's *A Theory of Justice* is still used to discuss current political and social issues. Scholars have asked what Rawls has to say with regard to global justice in an increasingly interconnected world. How does justice as fairness* relate to global environmental concerns? Which circumstances and reasons might determine a just war? Which moral issues are raised by the use of new military technologies, such as drones?

Rawls's work provides a robust analytical framework to reflect on possible answers to these questions. Many of the issues have been tackled in the scholarly literature that has emerged in response to *A Theory of Justice*.

Rawls's conception of fundamental rights has been criticized as minimalist. His work is primarily concerned with political and civil rights, and does not address redistributive principles such as social and economic rights. This omission provokes reactions from those scholars who think that inequality on a global scale is an injustice that political institutions have a moral obligation to address. The philosopher

> ❝ John Rawls's The Law of Peoples represents a culmination of his reflections on how we might reasonably and peacefully live together in a just world. My aim in this article is partly to pay homage by being more royalist than the king: I argue that Rawls's theory of justice can and should be extended ... The result is a conception of global justice that is more liberal in Rawls's own terms. ❞
>
> Andrew Kuper, "Rawlsian Global Justice: Beyond the Law of Peoples to a Cosmopolitan Law of Persons"

Thomas Pogge,* for example, has developed the idea of global redistributive tax*[1] and the empowerment of international institutions. The political theorist Charles Beitz*[2] has argued for the need to fully incorporate economic and social rights into universal human rights.* These ideas conflict with Rawls's minimalist theories of human rights. Rawls does not prescribe specific actions or institutions for promoting human rights. He simply advances a means for thinking about these issues rationally with the assumption that it is rational to believe that thinking about these issues will lead to them being advanced.

Schools of Thought

Rawls's work resulted in a school of thought referred to as "Rawlsian thought" or "Rawlsianism." In his biography of Rawls, Thomas Pogge provides a list of Rawls's most influential students. Many of them are among the most influential contemporary political thinkers;[3] it should be noted, however, that they often adjust, correct, or reinterpret important components of Rawls's theory to suit their own interests and arguments.

When *A Theory of Justice* was first published, globalization*—the convergence of global economies and cultures—and the interconnectedness of human existence were not as relevant as they became in the decades that followed. This is why the international dimension of *A Theory of Justice* is rather minimal. Rawlsian thinkers have built upon Rawls's theory, applying it to the global social and political spheres. Thinkers such as Beitz and Pogge disagree with Rawls's minimalism in global justice. Their cosmopolitan* theories— belonging to a branch of liberal* political theory characterized by a commitment to the idea of a universal form of citizenship—seek recognition for universal human rights in the civil, political, economic, and social spheres.

Rawls proposed a narrower conception of international justice; in his work, freedom is conceived as having universal appeal and equality is closely related to domestic politics. Thinkers such as Pogge, however, have advocated extending Rawls's principles of justice to the universal sphere, which has led to a theory of global redistributive justice.[4]

Rawls's work radically changed debate in the field of political theory. But while his theory is highly influential and has shaped the thinking of many scholars, the field of political theory has become somewhat fixated with Rawls's work; this perhaps might undermine its capacity to contribute to innovation.[5]

In Current Scholarship

Among scholars who identify Rawls as a primary influence on their thought are Charles Beitz, Thomas Pogge, the American philosophers Thomas Nagel,* Thomas Scanlon,* Joshua Cohen, Samuel Freeman,* and Paul Weithman,* and the Irish philosopher Onora O'Neill.* Cosmopolitan thinkers such as Beitz, the American philosopher Martha Nussbaum, and the British political theorist Simon Caney use his ideas to speak about issues of global justice. Much of this debate centers on whether Rawls's view of international justice, largely developed in his book *The Law of Peoples*, guarantees sufficient standards of justice. Another important scholar who has contributed to this debate is the influential Indian-born philosopher Amartya Sen,* who discusses the problem of inequality and how poverty can be measured.[6]

Although the issues of global justice and inequality have been addressed widely in the political debate, others, such as the issue of environmental preservation and the idea of intergenerational justice, are still emerging. The British philosopher Brian Barry* has discussed the limitations of Rawls's theory from the point of view of intergenerational issues—but this is a debate that will continue to be updated. Demands for justice will keep arising in new domestic and international political contexts.[7]

Similarly, although the question of a just war is centuries old, the "new wars" fought since 2000 pose new questions on the morality of war and its regulation; while Rawls does not address these questions directly, answers may be found through use of the conceptual framework that his theory provides.

NOTES

1   Thomas W. Pogge, "Eradicating Systemic Poverty: Brief for a Global Resources Dividend," *Journal of Human Development* 2, no. 1 (2001): 59–77.

2   Charles R. Beitz, *Political Theory and International Relations*, 2nd ed. (Princeton: Princeton University Press, 1999).

3   Thomas Winfried Pogge and Michelle Kosch, *John Rawls: His Life and Theory of Justice* (London: Oxford University Press, 2007), 24.

4   For a version of this proposal see Pogge, "Eradicating Systemic Poverty."

5   Consider, for example, the criticism raised by Berkowitz in this respect. Peter Berkowitz, "The Ambiguities of Rawls's Influence," *Perspectives on Politics* 4, no.1 (2006): 121–33.

6   Amartya Sen, *Inequality Reexamined* (Oxford: Clarendon Press, 1992) and *Development as Freedom* (Oxford: Oxford University Press, 2001).

7   Brian Barry, *Theories of Justice* (Hemel Hempstead: Harvester Wheatsheaf, 1989).

IMPACT AND INFLUENCE TODAY

KEY POINTS

- Although more than 40 years have passed since the publication of *A Theory of Justice*, it is cited in more publications in more fields of thought than ever before.

- A number of scholars remain unconvinced by Rawls's discussion of equality; they have sought to build their own innovative solutions to problems of equality.

- Even Rawls's harshest critics continue to cite his work as a theory that must be reckoned with.

Position

John Rawls's seminal work *A Theory of Justice* is perhaps more relevant now than it was when it was written.

In 2010 the leading political theorist Amartya Sen* published his acclaimed work *The Idea of Justice*[1]—a significant portion of which is dedicated to a discussion of Rawls's theory. Sen was a colleague of Rawls at Harvard. Their exchange of ideas went on for decades, producing some of the most important contributions to political theory in the contemporary scholarly debate. In *The Idea of Justice*, Sen proposes a thorough and innovative critique of Rawls's theory of justice. His main criticism of Rawls's thesis is that it defines justice in terms of perfect principles upon which a just society should rely. According to Sen, this "transcendental institutionalism" (that is, the assumptions it makes about the nature and role of the institution) should be abandoned; in its place there should be assessment and comparison of existing institutions and their social impact. He claims that thinkers such as Jeremy Bentham,* Adam Smith,* and Karl Marx*

> 66 The development of Western democracies in the twentieth century has placed increasingly severe strains on liberal concepts of social justice. Two major factors involved in this process are international competition with non-capitalist★ societies, and continual internal conflict between elites and the dispossessed ... Given these developments, it is not surprising that a book such as John Rawls's A Theory of Justice might touch off considerable controversy—perhaps more than any other work in social theory since Keynes' General Theory. 99
>
> Barry Clark and Herbert Gintis, "Rawlsian Justice and Economic Systems"

were already engaged in this process of comparison. Sen calls this "realization-focused comparison" and places himself in this tradition.

This rather pragmatic approach to the scholarly debate comes from Sen's underlying assumption that reasoning does not deliver the universal and incontrovertible principles that liberal* thinkers expect. This does not happen even under the conditions of the Rawlsian thought experiment* of the "original position."* Furthermore, even if reason did have the capacity to determine perfect principles of justice, human beings would not necessarily follow its dictates. Sen argues that injustice would therefore still take place. By proposing an alternative way to develop a theory of justice, Sen offers another contribution to the debate on Rawls. This may spark further reaction and continue to perpetuate the debate about justice in the field of political theory.

Interaction

Surprisingly, Rawls's work is not primarily challenged by the people he himself openly disagreed with—the utilitarians* and intuitionists.*

This may be because his book was so influential that these schools of thought fell out of fashion. But groups exist, on both sides of the political spectrum, that do not agree with Rawls's text.

One of Rawls's more famous critics is the American philosopher Robert Nozick.* Nozick's work *Anarchy, State, and Utopia*, published in 1974, is highly critical of Rawls. Nozick criticizes Rawls's ideas about social justice, especially the idea of redistribution. Nozick is a libertarian.* The main concern of libertarianism is the right of individuals to act autonomously and to avoid as many obligations and entanglements to society as possible. Nozick is against the idea of encouraging social equality through collecting taxes and distributing benefits. What for Rawls is social justice and in keeping with the difference principle,* for Nozick amounts to nothing but state-sanctioned theft.[2]

Coming from the opposite direction are Marxist* thinkers like the philosopher Gerald Cohen.* Like Nozick, Cohen is critical of Rawls's discussion of equality, but for the opposite reason. Cohen argues that the justice Rawls describes actually requires total equality. As a result Rawls's difference principle—which allows for different amounts of wealth and status if these inequalities benefit society—is actually a way of watering down his whole theory of justice.[3]

The Continuing Debate

Much of the debate that surrounds Rawls's work is concerned with whether the way he applies his ideas goes far enough, or how it can be applied in new ways or to new circumstances. Unsurprisingly, the focus of political theories changes as political issues change. This explains, at least in part, why Rawlsian ideas are now being debated in fields like economics and environmentalism.

Economic thinkers like Amartya Sen and the American scholar Nien-hê Hsieh* use Rawls's principles of justice to think about what is required to create a just economic order. Hsieh draws on *A Theory of*

Justice and on Rawls's later book *The Law of Peoples* to apply Rawlsian ideas to the issue of business ethics. He uses Rawlsian ideas to argue that transnational corporations—corporations that operate across international borders— have an obligation to assist people in developing economies. He suggests they should implement just policies such as labor rights and environmental protections.[4]

Recent environmental writing, like that of the Norwegian political theorist Oluf Langhelle,* applies Rawls's ideas to include environmental goods. This is similar to the way Rawls discusses economic goods and wealth in *A Theory of Justice*.[5] In doing this, Langhelle is following in the tradition of Charles Beitz,* who applied Rawlsian ideas to the issue of global social justice.

NOTES

1   Amartya Sen, *The Idea of Justice* (Cambridge, MA: Belknap Press of Harvard University Press, 2009).

2   Robert Nozick, "Distributive Justice," *Philosophy & Public Affairs* (1973): 79–81.

3   The most relevant critical observation on Rawls can be found in G. A. Cohen, *Rescuing Justice and Equality* (Cambridge, MA: Harvard University Press, 2008).

4   Nien-hê Hsieh, "The Obligations of Transnational Corporations: Rawlsian Justice and the Duty of Assistance," *Business Ethics Quarterly* 14, no. 4 (2004): 643.

5   Oluf Langhelle, "Sustainable Development and Social Justice: Expanding the Rawlsian Framework of Global Justice," *Environmental Values* 9, no. 3 (2000): 295–323.

WHERE NEXT?

KEY POINTS

- Rawls's *A Theory of Justice*, its related principles of fairness and limited equality, and its many analytical tools made it an instant classic.

- Interest in Rawls's work continues to be extremely high. Many political thinkers believe his text must be acknowledged in any discussion that touches upon its key themes.

- Thinkers interested in a wide array of issues now use Rawls's ideas about justice. These issues range from development* and human rights* to the environment.

Potential

The influence of John Rawls's seminal text *A Theory of Justice* has been enormous in its own field and in related academic contexts. More than 40 years after the book was published, political theorists call it one of the most significant (if not the most important) contributions to the field. Perhaps the clearest indication of Rawls's stature was accorded to him by one of his sharpest critics, the philosopher Gerald Cohen.*[1] Cohen commented that "at most two books in the history of Western political philosophy* have a claim to be regarded as greater than *A Theory of Justice*: Plato's* *Republic* and Hobbes's* *Leviathan*."[2] The works of the Ancient Greek philosopher Plato and the English philosopher Thomas Hobbes are not simply regarded as classics. They are seen as indispensable texts for understanding political societies and philosophy. For a critic to place Rawls in the company of great thinkers like these speaks volumes for Rawls's reputation as an original

> ❝ My hope is that justice as fairness* will seem reasonable and useful, even if not fully convincing, to a wide range of thoughtful political opinions and thereby express an essential part of the common core of the democratic tradition. ❞
>
> John Rawls, preface to the revised edition, *A Theory of Justice*

and challenging thinker.

The fields of moral philosophy, epistemology (the study of knowledge), and economics have also been significantly influenced by Rawls's theory. This is not surprising, as his ideas delve deeply into questions of morals. How should people and societies make judgments about what is morally right? However, Rawls himself stated that his theory only applies to the most fundamental structure of society.[3] This makes it hard to estimate the impact of *A Theory of Justice* in contexts outside political theory and its related fields.

Future Directions

The complexity of Rawls's theory means that his ideas continue to be reinterpreted and applied to new fields of study. Today, the Rawlsian school of thought is among the most influential of political theories. Even thinkers who have criticized Rawls engage with his ideas and with the way his ideas have been developed by Rawlsian thinkers.

Rawls's approach to justice continues to shape the way other thinkers deal with this concept and how it should govern society. Scholars from other disciplines also borrow from his work. Academics interested in sustainable development, for example, use the Rawlsian argument that acting in a sustainable way is the right—that is moral or fair—thing to do, both for people today and for future generations.

But not all of Rawls's ideas work perfectly in practice. Scholars of international politics have not yet found a way to reconcile the ideas held by different nation states about what is just or good. Nonetheless, Rawls's work resonates with the need to create universally acceptable norms within international affairs. The more human beings live, trade, work, and engage politically at a global level, the greater the need for a common understanding of what is meant by justice.

Summary

A Theory of Justice inspired and continues to inspire scholars from a number of fields interested in the idea of social justice. Philosophers, lawmakers, war protestors, human rights activists, and numerous other professionals have been inspired and challenged by Rawls. His original and highly open approach focuses on creating a society that best cares for all of its citizens. In contrast with many other political philosophers, Rawls shows his readers how to replicate his thinking. This allows them to imagine for themselves what institutions and practices are most likely to achieve a state that they would be willing to live in— even if they were at the bottom of the social ladder.

Although written in 1971, Rawls's thought experiments* and the concepts he derives from them are perhaps more useful now than ever. Issues such as globalization,* environmental degradation, the changing nature of employment, and the power of multinational corporations all need people to think about justice, equality, and fairness. As Rawls argues: "Justice is the first virtue of social institutions, as truth is of systems of thought."[4]

A Theory of Justice will remain a work that provides challenging ideas, philosophical reflection, and political and social inspiration to its readers.

NOTES

1 G. A. Cohen, *Rescuing Justice and Equality* (Cambridge, MA: Harvard University Press, 2008).

2 Cohen, *Rescuing Justice*, 11.

3 Louis-Philippe Hodgson, "Why the Basic Structure?" *Canadian Journal of Philosophy* 42, no. 3–4 (2012): 303–34.

4 Rawls, *A Theory of Justice*, 3.

GLOSSARY

GLOSSARY OF TERMS

Amnesty International: an international organization founded to support human rights (notably those of people imprisoned for their political beliefs).

Capitalism: an economic system that relies on markets to determine the supply and price of given goods. It assumes that people are rational actors who make decisions based on what benefits them most.

Categorical imperative: in the philosopher Immanuel Kant's moral theory, categorical imperatives correspond to the idea that certain moral duties are determined by our nature as rational moral beings and as such are always and universally (categorically) valid, ordering what we should do on the basis of a criterion of rationality.

Civil Rights Act: a 1964 law that formally forbade discrimination on the basis of sex and race in housing, employment, education, and other public settings in the United States. Crucially, it put in place a number of protections to ensure minorities would be able to vote in fair elections.

Civil rights movement: a struggle beginning in the 1950s in the United States to achieve racial justice and equality. Many of its key moments occurred in the 1960s, including the speeches of Malcolm X and Martin Luther King, Jr., as well as the passage of the Civil Rights Act.

Cold War (1947–89): a period of tension between the United States and the Soviet Union. While the two countries never engaged in direct military conflict, they engaged in covert and proxy wars and espionage against one another.

Communism: a political ideology that relies on the state ownership of the means of production, the collectivization of labor, and the abolition of social class.

Communitarianism: a current of political theory that emerged as a reaction to the rise of liberal political theory, especially after the publication of Rawls's *A Theory of Justice*. Communitarians are critical of various aspects of liberal individualism and in particular of the idea of an autonomous human being capable of developing a moral conception independently of the society and community to which they naturally belong.

Constitutionalism: the study of constitutions, particularly written constitutions, but also the belief that each state or society is governed by a certain basic set of values from which all other law is derived.

Contractarianism: a key branch of Western political theory. It is based on the idea that human beings agree on the condition of social life by becoming part of a hypothetical contract among themselves, in which they agree on the rules and conditions for living together in a society. Some of the main thinkers in this tradition are Thomas Hobbes (1588–1679), John Locke (1632–1704), Immanuel Kant (1724–1804), and Jean-Jacques Rousseau (1712–78).

Cosmopolitanism: a branch of liberal political theory particularly characterized by its universalism and commitment to the idea of a universal form of citizenship. The word "cosmopolitan" (which literally means "citizen of the world") dates back to classic Greek philosophy, when Stoic philosophers proposed the idea that humans are in fact citizens of the world.

Democratization: the process by which states give more power to their citizens in the organization of state institutions and the election of their leaders.

Development: also called human development, this is a field that promotes well-being in societies lacking economic, educational, and other resources required to be self-sufficient and minimally prosperous.

Difference principle (principle of difference): the second principle that Rawls lists in his theory of justice. This principle proposes that an unequal distribution of goods in a just society can be tolerated only as far as this distribution is beneficial to the least advantaged persons of that society and that they are attached to offices and positions that are open to all. This principle constitutes the egalitarian component of Rawls's theory of justice and is formulated in various forms across the book.

Enlightenment: a Western European intellectual current of the mid-1600s to the early 1800s characterized by a movement towards rationality over superstition and for its belief that education and knowledge could improve the human condition.

Global redistributive tax: a theoretical tax suggested by Thomas Pogge, which would allow the world to be more just by moving resources to those states and societies that have been previously disadvantaged or impoverished.

Globalization: the process by which political, cultural, and economic structures are becoming more unified around the world. Due to improvements in technology, travel, international business, and global media, many people argue that globalization is becoming more and more pronounced.

Hiroshima: with Nagasaki, the site of one of the two atomic bomb attacks in the history of warfare; both are Japanese cities. The use of the atomic bomb was seen as a necessary evil to force Japan to surrender and bring an end to World War II in the Pacific region. Scholars and society continue to fiercely debate the ethics and necessity of this action.

Holocaust: an event considered to be one of the low points of human history. During World War II, the Nazis and their collaborators killed over 11 million people in a systematized and highly organized fashion. Some six million of these people were killed simply for being Jewish. Other groups targeted for extermination included Roma ("gypsies"), homosexuals, and people suffering from physical and mental disabilities.

Human rights: generally argued to be universal, these are rights that exist simply by virtue of being human. Various laws and treaties exist to advance and protect these rights, which include things like the right to be a citizen, freedom to participate in government, fair trials, and so on.

Industrial Age: a period beginning in the mid–1700s and extending into the 1900s, which saw the rapid development of machinery, markets, mass production, and other technologies that radically transformed daily life and society.

Intuitionism: according to Rawls, "the doctrine that there is an irreducible family of first principles which have to be weighed against one another by asking ourselves which balance, in our considered judgment, is the most just." In intuitionism there is no priority rule or method that allows conflicts between one principle of justice and another to be balanced; this balancing between principles is to be done by intuition.

Justice as fairness: the conception according to which the principles that define justice are agreed upon on the basis of a procedure that would be considered fair by anyone, in the sense that they lead to conclusions that would be considered legitimate by any reasonable person, independent of any contingent aspect. To achieve the conditions of fairness, Rawls develops the thought experiment of the original position and its related concepts.

Kilei Ridge: A battle site in the Philippines where Rawls fought in World War II. It was here that he heard a sermon preached by a pastor who said that God directed the bullets of the Allied forces at the Japanese. This caused Rawls to deeply question, and ultimately reject, his Christian faith.

League of Women Voters: an organization in the United States founded to encourage women to claim positions of influence in the nation's civic structure. It was founded shortly after women in the United States were permitted to vote.

Liberalism: one of the most relevant political theories of Western culture. It has its foundations in the Enlightenment of the eighteenth century and is primarily linked to thinkers such as Immanuel Kant and John Locke, among others. Its historical foundation is linked with individual emancipation of free citizens especially in the French Revolution (1789)—a period of great political reform in France in which the monarchy was overthrown and government democratized. Its central concern is with the justification of political institutions that protect the individual freedom of the person against the interference of other persons and in particular political institutions and leaders.

Libertarianism: a sub-category of liberal political theory which is greatly concerned with the principles of individual freedom and especially negative freedom—the freedom of a person from external interferences. A key element of libertarian thinking is the inalienable right of the individual to property, which libertarians such as Robert Nozick consider of fundamental importance; for this reason, they criticize forms of distributive justice (the distribution of wealth with the aim of securing social justice).

Marxism: in general terms, Marxism includes all the theories derived from the work of Karl Marx, and in particular his greatly influential work *Capital*. Marxist theories include a wide range of different conceptions sharing a critique of the capitalist system, of its distribution of the means of production, of the institution of private property and of individualism, and proposing the idea of class struggle or social reform, the abolition of private property, and strong egalitarianism and redistribution among all members of society.

Nazis (National Socialist Party): a far-right political party led by Adolf Hitler, which ruled Germany from 1933 to 1945. They believed in a superior Aryan (Germanic) race and were responsible for systematically killing over 11 million people in the Holocaust. They were especially opposed to Jewish people, as well as the disabled, homosexuals, and Roma Gypsy people.

Original position: The original position is a thought experiment proposed by Rawls to justify the two principles that are established by his theory of justice. The thought experiment begins with the questions: If a rational person had a blank canvas to create a new society, what would they want that society to achieve? How could they best create a society that meets these goals?

Pluralism: a political system that can accommodate people from a number of different backgrounds, especially in terms of ethnicity or religion. It aims to provide equal rights for all citizens and to ensure that individuals are free to act according to their consciences, all while promoting social harmony between these groups.

Political philosophy: a subcategory of philosophy specifically concerned with developing theories about the social lives of human beings and the norms and institutions that regulate them. Philosophical speculation about politics is among the oldest. In the Western tradition, political philosophy goes back to the ancient Greek philosophers Plato and Aristotle.

Psychology: the study of the human mind and how it works to influence human beliefs, behaviors, and decisions.

Reflective equilibrium: a concept that describes the way in which persons develop their considered convictions of justice by going back and forth from their consolidated principles to reevaluated considerations and then reaching a point of equilibrium.

Social contract: the idea that society creates a state and gives up some individual freedoms in exchange for security and the protection of predefined political rights.

Soviet Union: the Union of Soviet Socialist Republics (USSR), a centralized Marxist-Leninist state made up of several sub-nations between 1922 and 1991.

State of nature: an imagined representation of how human society would be in its natural state, without government interference. Hobbes famously argued it would be violent and terrible; thinkers like Rousseau argue people are naturally peaceful.

Teleology: a view of knowledge that believes in a predefined end or goal to history.

Thought experiments: tools used by philosophers to create an imaginary situation that allows them to prove a particular point is logical or a certain conclusion would be likely in a given set of circumstances. Examples include Hobbes's "state of nature" and Rawls's "original position."

Toleration: a political value that argues that society should accept differences that do not cause material harm to other individuals.

Utilitarianism: a theory according to which utility and happiness should be the main criteria of judgment for moral decisions, and these should be considered in an aggregated measure when thinking of societies, so justifying policies that may maximize collective utility but are detrimental to individual rights and well-being.

Veil of ignorance: an imaginary condition under which the person operating in the original position makes decisions and reasons about justice, not knowing their social condition, such as social status or class; their natural gifts, such as intelligence, strengths, or abilities; or their individual moral preferences.

Vietnam War: a Cold War conflict that took place between 1955 and 1975. Considered one of the most controversial events in contemporary US history, it has profoundly influenced the political debate in the United States.

World War II: a conflict fought in the years 1939–1945 that involved virtually every major country on earth. Fought between the Allies (the United States, Britain, France, the Soviet Union and others), and the

Axis (Germany, Italy and Japan, along with their allies), it was seen as a major moral struggle between freedom and tyranny and included seminal events like the Holocaust.

PEOPLE MENTIONED IN THE TEXT

Brian Barry (1936–2009) was a British philosopher who taught at the London School of Economics and Columbia University. Although friends with Rawls, he critiqued his work in the well-regarded book *The Liberal Critique of Justice* (1972).

Charles Beitz (b. 1949) is an American political theorist who has written several studies on human rights and issues of global justice. One of his most influential publications is *Political Theory and International Relations*, in which he proposes a cosmopolitan political theory.

Jeremy Bentham (1748–1832) is the most famous thinker of utilitarianism. His maxim that society should strive to achieve the "greatest good for the greatest number" was highly influential in political and philosophical movements for over 100 years following his death. He was active in a number of social spheres, including prison reform, education, and welfare.

Isaiah Berlin (1909–97) was a prominent figure of liberal thought in the English-speaking world and elsewhere. He is most commonly known for his distinction between negative and positive freedom, among other contributions to the discipline.

Bill Clinton (b. 1946) was the 42nd president of the United States. His approach to government and social justice would have made him sympathetic to many of Rawls's aims.

Gerald Cohen (1941–2009) was an influential Marxist philosopher, the author of several publications that were critical of liberal political theory from a socialist perspective. His work is extensive but some of the most relevant critical observation on Rawls can be found in *Rescuing Justice and Equality* (2008).

Samuel Freeman is a professor at Pennsylvania University and author of several publications, including one of the most popular commentaries on Rawls's philosophical work, *Rawls* (2007).

Stuart Hampshire (1914–2004) was an influential philosopher and political thinker known for various publications, such as his study of Spinoza, and his anti-rationalist views on public ethics, expressed in *Thought and Action* and *Justice Is Conflict*.

Jonathan Harrison (1924–2014) was an English philosopher who taught at a number of universities. He is well known for his book *Our Knowledge of Right and Wrong*.

Henry Roy Forbes Harrod (1900–1978) was an English economist who created a number of novel theories in response to economic liberalism. He also is famous for his biography of the economist John Maynard Keynes.

Herbert Lionel Adolphus Hart (1907–92) was an influential philosopher of the law based in Oxford and then at the London School of Economics and Political Science, among other major academic centers. He is the author of one of the earliest replies to Rawls's theories.

Thomas Hobbes (1588–1679) was an English philosopher whose major work, *Leviathan*, famously used the thought experiment of a "state of nature" where people live without a state to argue that such a situation would be the worst possible for society. Instead, he advocates the creation of a social contract in which people living in total freedom willingly give up some of that freedom to a sovereign power in order to gain order and security.

Nien-hê Hsieh is an associate professor of business administration at Harvard Business School. His work considers questions such as whether profit-seeking corporations can be good for society.

David Hume (1711–76) was one of the most important philosophers of the Scottish Enlightenment. He argued that people should base their morality on the usefulness, or utility, of their actions in achieving pleasure or gain for themselves and society. In this sense, he is the founder of the utilitarian school of political philosophy.

Lyndon B. Johnson (1908–73) was the 36th president of the United States. He came to power after the assassination of President Kennedy and continued many of his policies, including the Vietnam War, which he greatly expanded, and the extension of civil rights for racial minorities.

Immanuel Kant (1724–1804) was one of the founding fathers of Western modern philosophical thought, known for a number of crucial publications and epitomizing the Enlightenment tradition. He was a forceful proponent of rationality, argued in favor of the need for republican government, and advocated individual political rights.

Oluf Langhelle is a professor at the University of Stavanger in Norway. He studies sustainable development, corporate social responsibility, political theory, globalization, and a number of other topics that relate to many of Rawls's concerns.

John Locke (1632–1704) was one of the most influential thinkers of the English-speaking world and of the Enlightenment well known for several intellectual contributions, including the *Two Treatises on Government* (1689).

Alasdair MacIntyre (b. 1929) is a philosopher especially known for his clear communitarian stance, presented in *After Virtue* and then developed further in subsequent publications.

Norman Malcolm (1911–90) was an American philosopher. He worked with Ludwig Wittgenstein while at Cambridge University.

Karl Marx (1818–83) was a famous German political thinker and writer who created the political theory of Marxism. His ideas are also referred to as communism. Using economic ideas about society, he argued that the working class should create a worldwide revolution against the property-owning class, seize the capital used to produce goods, and own them jointly as a community. Then all would be provided for equally from community assets.

Thomas Nagel (b. 1937) is an influential political philosopher at New York University, known for several of his publications on political theory and philosophy, and especially for his critique of reductionism.

Onora O'Neill (b. 1941) is an influential Kantian philosopher, now also a member of the House of Lords and a professor at the University of Cambridge.

Robert Nozick (1938–2002) was an important political theorist primarily associated with the liberal sub-class of libertarianism. He was the author of a debated critique of Rawls's theory, critical of principles of social justice and redistribution above all.

Plato (429–347 B.C.E.) is one of the most influential and famous philosophers of all time. His book *The Republic* has been a major influence on political thinkers ever since antiquity. Amongst his most important political ideas are that it is possible to imagine an ideal state that can advance a pre-defined "good life."

Thomas Pogge (b. 1953) is a professor of political science at Columbia University and one of the youngest students of Rawls. He is known for his theory of global justice, advocating principles of global redistribution.

Jean-Jacques Rousseau (1712–78) was a leading thinker of the Enlightenment, and among the inspirational sources of the French Revolution. His political-theory work of highest relevance is about the idea of the social contract.

Michael Sandel (b. 1953) is an American political philosopher at Harvard University. He is best known for his critique of Rawls's theory of justice in *Liberalism and the Limits of Justice* (1998). More recently, he became popular for an innovative course on justice which has been widely publicized in the media and is also available online.

Thomas Scanlon (b. 1940) is the Alford Professor of Natural Religion, Moral Philosophy, and Civil Polity at Harvard University. He is one of the leading scholars of moral and political philosophy, although his initial academic training was in mathematics. Among his most influential publications are *The Difficulty of Tolerance: Essays in Political Philosophy* (2003) and *What We Owe to Each Other* (1998).

Amartya Sen (b. 1933) is a philosopher and an economist, a Nobel Prize laureate who has published extensively on a number of topics, often at the crossroads between philosophy and economics. He is known as the founder of the idea of human development and the "capability approach," which have subsequently become influential in the assessment of poverty at the United Nations. One of his most recent works is a comprehensive treatise on justice in which he presents several arguments critical of Rawls's theory.

Judith Shklar (1928–92) was a political theorist at Harvard University. In her work she wrote about injustice, political evils, and the "liberalism of fear."

Henry Sidgwick (1838–1900) was an English philosopher in the utilitarian tradition. His work is often seen as the most sophisticated development of the earlier thought of people like Bentham, who shared his belief that society must strive to provide "the greatest good for the greatest number."

Adam Smith (1723–90) was a Scottish philosopher and arguably the father of modern economics. His most famous work, *The Wealth of Nations*, speaks about the market as the "invisible hand" which helps to ensure that goods are distributed as efficiently as possible in society. His work is central to many politically liberal concepts about the relationship between the state, business, and citizens.

Charles Taylor (b. 1931) is one the most influential contemporary philosophers, known particularly for his work on Hegel. His critique of liberal political theory can be found in *Human Agency and Language: Philosophical Papers 1* (1985).

Paul Weithman is professor of political philosophy at the University of Notre Dame. He has studied at Harvard under the direction of Rawls and Shklar and is the author of several publications on political theory, particularly on Rawls's political liberalism.

Ludwig Wittgenstein (1889–1951) was an Austrian philosopher who was especially interested in the role that language plays in human thought, its possibilities, and its limits.

WORKS CITED

WORKS CITED

Barry, Brian. *The Liberal Theory of Justice: A Critical Examination of the Principal Doctrines in "A Theory of Justice" by John Rawls*. Oxford: Clarendon Press, 1973.

— — —. *Theories of Justice*. Hemel Hempstead: Harvester Wheatsheaf, 1989.

Beitz, Charles R. *The Idea of Human Rights*. Oxford: Oxford University Press, 2009.

— — —. *Political Theory and International Relations*, 2nd ed. Princeton, N.J.: Princeton University Press, 1999.

Berkowitz, Peter. "The Ambiguities of Rawls's Influence." *Perspectives on Politics* 4, no. 1 (2006): 121–33.

Berlin, Isaiah, and Henry Hardy. *The Crooked Timber of Humanity: Chapters in the History of Ideas*. London: John Murray, 1990.

Brown, Chris. "On Amartya Sen and the *Idea of Justice*." *Ethics & International Affairs* 24, no. 3 (2010): 309–18.

Buckler, Steve, and David P. Dolowitz. "Theorizing the Third Way: New Labour and Social Justice." *Journal of Political Ideologies* 5, no. 3 (2000): 301–20.

Caney, Simon. *Justice beyond Borders: A Global Political Theory*. Oxford: Oxford University Press, 2005.

Clark, Barry, and Herbert Gintis. "Rawlsian Justice and Economic Systems." *Philosophy & Public Affairs* (1978): 302–25.

Clinton, William J. *Public Papers of Presidents of the United States*: *William J. Clinton* (1999).

Cohen, G. A. *Rescuing Justice and Equality*. Cambridge, MA: Harvard University Press, 2008.

Freeman, Samuel Richard. *Rawls*. London: Routledge, 2007.

Gregory, Eric. "Before the Original Position: The Neo Orthodox Theology of the Young John Rawls." *Journal of Religious Ethics* 35, no. 2 (2007): 195–6.

Hampshire, Stuart. *Spinoza*. Harmondsworth: Pelican; New York: Penguin, 1988.

— — —. *Thought and Action*. London: Chatto & Windus, 1959.

Hart, H. L. A. *The Concept of Law*. Oxford: Clarendon Press, 1961.

— — —. "Rawls on Liberty and Its Priority." *University of Chicago Law Review* 40, no. 3 (1973): 534–55.

Hodgson, Louis-Philippe. "Why the Basic Structure?" *Canadian Journal of Philosophy* 42, no. 3–4 (2012): 303–4.

Hsieh, Nien-hê. "The Obligations of Transnational Corporations: Rawlsian Justice and the Duty of Assistance." *Business Ethics Quarterly* 14, no. 4 (2004): 643–61.

Kuper, Andrew. "Rawlsian Global Justice: Beyond the Law of Peoples to a Cosmopolitan Law of Persons." *Political Theory* 28, no. 5 (2000): 640–74.

Langhelle, Oluf. "Sustainable Development and Social Justice: Expanding the Rawlsian Framework of Global Justice." *Environmental Values* 9, no. 3 (2000): 295–323.

Locke, John. *Locke on Toleration*. Edited by Richard Vernon. Cambridge: Cambridge University Press, 2010.

— — —. *Two Treatises of Government*. Edited by Peter Laslett. Cambridge: Cambridge University Press, 1988.

MacIntyre, Alasdair C. *After Virtue: A Study in Moral Theory*, 3rd ed. Notre Dame, IN: University of Notre Dame Press, 2007.

— — —. *Whose Justice? Which Rationality?* London: Duckworth, 1988.

Nagel, Thomas. "The Problem of Global Justice." *Philosophy & Public Affairs* 33, no. 2 (2005): 113–47.

Nozick, Robert. "Distributive Justice." *Philosophy & Public Affairs* 3, no. 1 (1973): 45–126.

— — —. *Anarchy, State, and Utopia*. Oxford: Blackwell, 1974.

Pogge, Thomas W. "Eradicating Systemic Poverty: Brief for a Global Resources Dividend." *Journal of Human Development* 2, no. 1 (2001): 59–77.

— — —. *Realizing Rawls*. Ithaca, N.Y.: Cornell University Press, 1989.

— — —. *World Poverty and Human Rights: Cosmopolitan Responsibilities and Reforms*, 2nd ed. Cambridge: Polity, 2008.

Pogge, Thomas, and Michelle Kosch. *John Rawls: His Life and Theory of Justice*. Oxford: Oxford University Press, 2007.

Rawls, John. *Collected Papers*. Edited by Samuel Richard Freeman. Cambridge, MA: Harvard University Press, 1999.

— — —. "50 Years after Hiroshima." *Dissent* (summer 1995): 323–7.

— — —. "Justice as Fairness." *Philosophical Review* 67, no. 2 (1958): 164–94.

— — —. *The Law of Peoples: With "The Idea of Public Reason Revisited"*. Cambridge, MA: Harvard University Press, 1999.

— — —. *Political Liberalism*. New York: Columbia University Press, 1993.

— — —. *A Theory of Justice*, rev. ed. Cambridge, MA: Belknap Press of Harvard University Press, 1999.

Rousseau, Jean-Jacques. *The Social Contract and Other Later Political Writings*. Edited by Victor Gourevitch. Cambridge: Cambridge University Press, 1997.

Sandel, Michael J. *Liberalism and the Limits of Justice*, 2nd ed. Cambridge: Cambridge University Press, 1998.

— — —. "The Procedural Republic and the Unencumbered Self." *Political Theory* 12, no. 1 (1984): 81–96.

Scanlon, Thomas. *The Difficulty of Tolerance: Essays in Political Philosophy*. Cambridge: Cambridge University Press, 2003.

— — —. *What We Owe to Each Other*. Cambridge, MA: Belknap Press of Harvard University Press, 1998.

Sen, Amartya. *Development as Freedom*. Oxford: Oxford University Press, 2001.

— — —. *The Idea of Justice*. Cambridge, MA: Belknap Press of Harvard University Press, 2009.

— — —. *Inequality Reexamined*. Oxford: Clarendon Press, 1992.

Shklar, Judith. "Giving Injustice Its Due." *Yale Law Journal* 98, no. 6 (1989): 1135–51.

Shklar, Judith N., and Stanley Hoffmann. *Political Thought and Political Thinkers*. Chicago: University of Chicago Press, 1998.

Taylor, Charles. *Human Agency and Language: Philosophical Papers 1*. Cambridge: Cambridge University Press, 1985.

Weithman, Paul J. *Why Political Liberalism? On John Rawls's Political Turn*. New York: Oxford University Press, 2011.

THE MACAT LIBRARY
BY DISCIPLINE

AFRICANA STUDIES

Chinua Achebe's *An Image of Africa: Racism in Conrad's Heart of Darkness*
W. E. B. Du Bois's *The Souls of Black Folk*
Zora Neale Huston's *Characteristics of Negro Expression*
Martin Luther King Jr's *Why We Can't Wait*
Toni Morrison's *Playing in the Dark: Whiteness in the American Literary Imagination*

ANTHROPOLOGY

Arjun Appadurai's *Modernity at Large: Cultural Dimensions of Globalisation*
Philippe Ariès's *Centuries of Childhood*
Franz Boas's *Race, Language and Culture*
Kim Chan & Renée Mauborgne's *Blue Ocean Strategy*
Jared Diamond's *Guns, Germs & Steel: the Fate of Human Societies*
Jared Diamond's *Collapse: How Societies Choose to Fail or Survive*
E. E. Evans-Pritchard's *Witchcraft, Oracles and Magic Among the Azande*
James Ferguson's *The Anti-Politics Machine*
Clifford Geertz's *The Interpretation of Cultures*
David Graeber's *Debt: the First 5000 Years*
Karen Ho's *Liquidated: An Ethnography of Wall Street*
Geert Hofstede's *Culture's Consequences: Comparing Values, Behaviors, Institutes and Organizations across Nations*
Claude Lévi-Strauss's *Structural Anthropology*
Jay Macleod's *Ain't No Makin' It: Aspirations and Attainment in a Low-Income Neighborhood*
Saba Mahmood's *The Politics of Piety: The Islamic Revival and the Feminist Subjec*t
Marcel Mauss's *The Gift*

BUSINESS

Jean Lave & Etienne Wenger's *Situated Learning*
Theodore Levitt's *Marketing Myopia*
Burton G. Malkiel's *A Random Walk Down Wall Street*
Douglas McGregor's *The Human Side of Enterprise*
Michael Porter's *Competitive Strategy: Creating and Sustaining Superior Performance*
John Kotter's *Leading Change*
C. K. Prahalad & Gary Hamel's *The Core Competence of the Corporation*

CRIMINOLOGY

Michelle Alexander's *The New Jim Crow: Mass Incarceration in the Age of Colorblindness*
Michael R. Gottfredson & Travis Hirschi's *A General Theory of Crime*
Richard Herrnstein & Charles A. Murray's *The Bell Curve: Intelligence and Class Structure in American Life*
Elizabeth Loftus's *Eyewitness Testimony*
Jay Macleod's *Ain't No Makin' It: Aspirations and Attainment in a Low-Income Neighborhood*
Philip Zimbardo's *The Lucifer Effect*

ECONOMICS

Janet Abu-Lughod's *Before European Hegemony*
Ha-Joon Chang's *Kicking Away the Ladder*
David Brion Davis's *The Problem of Slavery in the Age of Revolution*
Milton Friedman's *The Role of Monetary Policy*
Milton Friedman's *Capitalism and Freedom*
David Graeber's *Debt: the First 5000 Years*
Friedrich Hayek's *The Road to Serfdom*
Karen Ho's *Liquidated: An Ethnography of Wall Street*

John Maynard Keynes's *The General Theory of Employment, Interest and Money*
Charles P. Kindleberger's *Manias, Panics and Crashes*
Robert Lucas's *Why Doesn't Capital Flow from Rich to Poor Countries?*
Burton G. Malkiel's *A Random Walk Down Wall Street*
Thomas Robert Malthus's *An Essay on the Principle of Population*
Karl Marx's *Capital*
Thomas Piketty's *Capital in the Twenty-First Century*
Amartya Sen's *Development as Freedom*
Adam Smith's *The Wealth of Nations*
Nassim Nicholas Taleb's *The Black Swan: The Impact of the Highly Improbable*
Amos Tversky's & Daniel Kahneman's *Judgment under Uncertainty: Heuristics and Biases*
Mahbub Ul Haq's *Reflections on Human Development*
Max Weber's *The Protestant Ethic and the Spirit of Capitalism*

FEMINISM AND GENDER STUDIES

Judith Butler's *Gender Trouble*
Simone De Beauvoir's *The Second Sex*
Michel Foucault's *History of Sexuality*
Betty Friedan's *The Feminine Mystique*
Saba Mahmood's *The Politics of Piety: The Islamic Revival and the Feminist Subjec*t
Joan Wallach Scott's *Gender and the Politics of History*
Mary Wollstonecraft's *A Vindication of the Rights of Woman*
Virginia Woolf's *A Room of One's Own*

GEOGRAPHY

The Brundtland Report's *Our Common Future*
Rachel Carson's *Silent Spring*
Charles Darwin's *On the Origin of Species*
James Ferguson's *The Anti-Politics Machine*
Jane Jacobs's *The Death and Life of Great American Cities*
James Lovelock's *Gaia: A New Look at Life on Earth*
Amartya Sen's *Development as Freedom*
Mathis Wackernagel & William Rees's *Our Ecological Footprint*

HISTORY

Janet Abu-Lughod's *Before European Hegemony*
Benedict Anderson's *Imagined Communities*
Bernard Bailyn's *The Ideological Origins of the American Revolution*
Hanna Batatu's *The Old Social Classes And The Revolutionary Movements Of Iraq*
Christopher Browning's *Ordinary Men: Reserve Police Batallion 101 and the Final Solution in Poland*
Edmund Burke's *Reflections on the Revolution in France*
William Cronon's *Nature's Metropolis: Chicago And The Great West*
Alfred W. Crosby's *The Columbian Exchange*
Hamid Dabashi's *Iran: A People Interrupted*
David Brion Davis's *The Problem of Slavery in the Age of Revolution*
Nathalie Zemon Davis's *The Return of Martin Guerre*
Jared Diamond's *Guns, Germs & Steel: the Fate of Human Societies*
Frank Dikotter's *Mao's Great Famine*
John W Dower's *War Without Mercy: Race And Power In The Pacific War*
W. E. B. Du Bois's *The Souls of Black Folk*
Richard J. Evans's *In Defence of History*
Lucien Febvre's *The Problem of Unbelief in the 16th Century*
Sheila Fitzpatrick's *Everyday Stalinism*

The Macat Library By Discipline

Eric Foner's *Reconstruction: America's Unfinished Revolution, 1863-1877*
Michel Foucault's *Discipline and Punish*
Michel Foucault's *History of Sexuality*
Francis Fukuyama's *The End of History and the Last Man*
John Lewis Gaddis's *We Now Know: Rethinking Cold War History*
Ernest Gellner's *Nations and Nationalism*
Eugene Genovese's *Roll, Jordan, Roll: The World the Slaves Made*
Carlo Ginzburg's *The Night Battles*
Daniel Goldhagen's *Hitler's Willing Executioners*
Jack Goldstone's *Revolution and Rebellion in the Early Modern World*
Antonio Gramsci's *The Prison Notebooks*
Alexander Hamilton, John Jay & James Madison's *The Federalist Papers*
Christopher Hill's *The World Turned Upside Down*
Carole Hillenbrand's *The Crusades: Islamic Perspectives*
Thomas Hobbes's *Leviathan*
Eric Hobsbawm's *The Age Of Revolution*
John A. Hobson's *Imperialism: A Study*
Albert Hourani's *History of the Arab Peoples*
Samuel P. Huntington's *The Clash of Civilizations and the Remaking of World Order*
C. L. R. James's *The Black Jacobins*
Tony Judt's *Postwar: A History of Europe Since 1945*
Ernst Kantorowicz's *The King's Two Bodies: A Study in Medieval Political Theology*
Paul Kennedy's *The Rise and Fall of the Great Powers*
Ian Kershaw's *The "Hitler Myth": Image and Reality in the Third Reich*
John Maynard Keynes's *The General Theory of Employment, Interest and Money*
Charles P. Kindleberger's *Manias, Panics and Crashes*
Martin Luther King Jr's *Why We Can't Wait*
Henry Kissinger's *World Order: Reflections on the Character of Nations and the Course of History*
Thomas Kuhn's *The Structure of Scientific Revolutions*
Georges Lefebvre's *The Coming of the French Revolution*
John Locke's *Two Treatises of Government*
Niccolò Machiavelli's *The Prince*
Thomas Robert Malthus's *An Essay on the Principle of Population*
Mahmood Mamdani's *Citizen and Subject: Contemporary Africa And The Legacy Of Late Colonialism*
Karl Marx's *Capital*
Stanley Milgram's *Obedience to Authority*
John Stuart Mill's *On Liberty*
Thomas Paine's *Common Sense*
Thomas Paine's *Rights of Man*
Geoffrey Parker's *Global Crisis: War, Climate Change and Catastrophe in the Seventeenth Century*
Jonathan Riley-Smith's *The First Crusade and the Idea of Crusading*
Jean-Jacques Rousseau's *The Social Contract*
Joan Wallach Scott's *Gender and the Politics of History*
Theda Skocpol's *States and Social Revolutions*
Adam Smith's *The Wealth of Nations*
Timothy Snyder's *Bloodlands: Europe Between Hitler and Stalin*
Sun Tzu's *The Art of War*
Keith Thomas's *Religion and the Decline of Magic*
Thucydides's *The History of the Peloponnesian War*
Frederick Jackson Turner's *The Significance of the Frontier in American History*
Odd Arne Westad's *The Global Cold War: Third World Interventions And The Making Of Our Times*

LITERATURE

Chinua Achebe's *An Image of Africa: Racism in Conrad's Heart of Darkness*
Roland Barthes's *Mythologies*
Homi K. Bhabha's *The Location of Culture*
Judith Butler's *Gender Trouble*
Simone De Beauvoir's *The Second Sex*
Ferdinand De Saussure's *Course in General Linguistics*
T. S. Eliot's *The Sacred Wood: Essays on Poetry and Criticism*
Zora Neale Huston's *Characteristics of Negro Expression*
Toni Morrison's *Playing in the Dark: Whiteness in the American Literary Imagination*
Edward Said's *Orientalism*
Gayatri Chakravorty Spivak's *Can the Subaltern Speak?*
Mary Wollstonecraft's *A Vindication of the Rights of Women*
Virginia Woolf's *A Room of One's Own*

PHILOSOPHY

Elizabeth Anscombe's *Modern Moral Philosophy*
Hannah Arendt's *The Human Condition*
Aristotle's *Metaphysics*
Aristotle's *Nicomachean Ethics*
Edmund Gettier's *Is Justified True Belief Knowledge?*
Georg Wilhelm Friedrich Hegel's *Phenomenology of Spirit*
David Hume's *Dialogues Concerning Natural Religion*
David Hume's *The Enquiry for Human Understanding*
Immanuel Kant's *Religion within the Boundaries of Mere Reason*
Immanuel Kant's *Critique of Pure Reason*
Søren Kierkegaard's *The Sickness Unto Death*
Søren Kierkegaard's *Fear and Trembling*
C. S. Lewis's *The Abolition of Man*
Alasdair MacIntyre's *After Virtue*
Marcus Aurelius's *Meditations*
Friedrich Nietzsche's *On the Genealogy of Morality*
Friedrich Nietzsche's *Beyond Good and Evil*
Plato's *Republic*
Plato's *Symposium*
Jean-Jacques Rousseau's *The Social Contract*
Gilbert Ryle's *The Concept of Mind*
Baruch Spinoza's *Ethics*
Sun Tzu's *The Art of War*
Ludwig Wittgenstein's *Philosophical Investigations*

POLITICS

Benedict Anderson's *Imagined Communities*
Aristotle's *Politics*
Bernard Bailyn's *The Ideological Origins of the American Revolution*
Edmund Burke's *Reflections on the Revolution in France*
John C. Calhoun's *A Disquisition on Government*
Ha-Joon Chang's *Kicking Away the Ladder*
Hamid Dabashi's *Iran: A People Interrupted*
Hamid Dabashi's *Theology of Discontent: The Ideological Foundation of the Islamic Revolution in Iran*
Robert Dahl's *Democracy and its Critics*
Robert Dahl's *Who Governs?*
David Brion Davis's *The Problem of Slavery in the Age of Revolution*

The Macat Library By Discipline

Alexis De Tocqueville's *Democracy in America*
James Ferguson's *The Anti-Politics Machine*
Frank Dikotter's *Mao's Great Famine*
Sheila Fitzpatrick's *Everyday Stalinism*
Eric Foner's *Reconstruction: America's Unfinished Revolution, 1863-1877*
Milton Friedman's *Capitalism and Freedom*
Francis Fukuyama's *The End of History and the Last Man*
John Lewis Gaddis's *We Now Know: Rethinking Cold War History*
Ernest Gellner's *Nations and Nationalism*
David Graeber's *Debt: the First 5000 Years*
Antonio Gramsci's *The Prison Notebooks*
Alexander Hamilton, John Jay & James Madison's *The Federalist Papers*
Friedrich Hayek's *The Road to Serfdom*
Christopher Hill's *The World Turned Upside Down*
Thomas Hobbes's *Leviathan*
John A. Hobson's *Imperialism: A Study*
Samuel P. Huntington's *The Clash of Civilizations and the Remaking of World Order*
Tony Judt's *Postwar: A History of Europe Since 1945*
David C. Kang's *China Rising: Peace, Power and Order in East Asia*
Paul Kennedy's *The Rise and Fall of Great Powers*
Robert Keohane's *After Hegemony*
Martin Luther King Jr.'s *Why We Can't Wait*
Henry Kissinger's *World Order: Reflections on the Character of Nations and the Course of History*
John Locke's *Two Treatises of Government*
Niccolò Machiavelli's *The Prince*
Thomas Robert Malthus's *An Essay on the Principle of Population*
Mahmood Mamdani's *Citizen and Subject: Contemporary Africa And The Legacy Of Late Colonialism*
Karl Marx's *Capital*
John Stuart Mill's *On Liberty*
John Stuart Mill's *Utilitarianism*
Hans Morgenthau's *Politics Among Nations*
Thomas Paine's *Common Sense*
Thomas Paine's *Rights of Man*
Thomas Piketty's *Capital in the Twenty-First Century*
Robert D. Putman's *Bowling Alone*
John Rawls's *Theory of Justice*
Jean-Jacques Rousseau's *The Social Contract*
Theda Skocpol's *States and Social Revolutions*
Adam Smith's *The Wealth of Nations*
Sun Tzu's *The Art of War*
Henry David Thoreau's *Civil Disobedience*
Thucydides's *The History of the Peloponnesian War*
Kenneth Waltz's *Theory of International Politics*
Max Weber's *Politics as a Vocation*
Odd Arne Westad's *The Global Cold War: Third World Interventions And The Making Of Our Times*

POSTCOLONIAL STUDIES

Roland Barthes's *Mythologies*
Frantz Fanon's *Black Skin, White Masks*
Homi K. Bhabha's *The Location of Culture*
Gustavo Gutiérrez's *A Theology of Liberation*
Edward Said's *Orientalism*
Gayatri Chakravorty Spivak's *Can the Subaltern Speak?*

PSYCHOLOGY

Gordon Allport's *The Nature of Prejudice*
Alan Baddeley & Graham Hitch's *Aggression: A Social Learning Analysis*
Albert Bandura's *Aggression: A Social Learning Analysis*
Leon Festinger's *A Theory of Cognitive Dissonance*
Sigmund Freud's *The Interpretation of Dreams*
Betty Friedan's *The Feminine Mystique*
Michael R. Gottfredson & Travis Hirschi's *A General Theory of Crime*
Eric Hoffer's *The True Believer: Thoughts on the Nature of Mass Movements*
William James's *Principles of Psychology*
Elizabeth Loftus's *Eyewitness Testimony*
A. H. Maslow's *A Theory of Human Motivation*
Stanley Milgram's *Obedience to Authority*
Steven Pinker's *The Better Angels of Our Nature*
Oliver Sacks's *The Man Who Mistook His Wife For a Hat*
Richard Thaler & Cass Sunstein's *Nudge: Improving Decisions About Health, Wealth and Happiness*
Amos Tversky's *Judgment under Uncertainty: Heuristics and Biases*
Philip Zimbardo's *The Lucifer Effect*

SCIENCE

Rachel Carson's *Silent Spring*
William Cronon's *Nature's Metropolis: Chicago And The Great West*
Alfred W. Crosby's *The Columbian Exchange*
Charles Darwin's *On the Origin of Species*
Richard Dawkin's *The Selfish Gene*
Thomas Kuhn's *The Structure of Scientific Revolutions*
Geoffrey Parker's *Global Crisis: War, Climate Change and Catastrophe in the Seventeenth Century*
Mathis Wackernagel & William Rees's *Our Ecological Footprint*

SOCIOLOGY

Michelle Alexander's *The New Jim Crow: Mass Incarceration in the Age of Colorblindness*
Gordon Allport's *The Nature of Prejudice*
Albert Bandura's *Aggression: A Social Learning Analysis*
Hanna Batatu's *The Old Social Classes And The Revolutionary Movements Of Iraq*
Ha-Joon Chang's *Kicking Away the Ladder*
W. E. B. Du Bois's *The Souls of Black Folk*
Émile Durkheim's *On Suicide*
Frantz Fanon's *Black Skin, White Masks*
Frantz Fanon's *The Wretched of the Earth*
Eric Foner's *Reconstruction: America's Unfinished Revolution, 1863-1877*
Eugene Genovese's *Roll, Jordan, Roll: The World the Slaves Made*
Jack Goldstone's *Revolution and Rebellion in the Early Modern World*
Antonio Gramsci's *The Prison Notebooks*
Richard Herrnstein & Charles A Murray's *The Bell Curve: Intelligence and Class Structure in American Life*
Eric Hoffer's *The True Believer: Thoughts on the Nature of Mass Movements*
Jane Jacobs's *The Death and Life of Great American Cities*
Robert Lucas's *Why Doesn't Capital Flow from Rich to Poor Countries?*
Jay Macleod's *Ain't No Makin' It: Aspirations and Attainment in a Low Income Neighborhood*
Elaine May's *Homeward Bound: American Families in the Cold War Era*
Douglas McGregor's *The Human Side of Enterprise*
C. Wright Mills's *The Sociological Imagination*

The Macat Library By Discipline

Thomas Piketty's *Capital in the Twenty-First Century*
Robert D. Putman's *Bowling Alone*
David Riesman's *The Lonely Crowd: A Study of the Changing American Character*
Edward Said's *Orientalism*
Joan Wallach Scott's *Gender and the Politics of History*
Theda Skocpol's *States and Social Revolutions*
Max Weber's *The Protestant Ethic and the Spirit of Capitalism*

THEOLOGY

Augustine's *Confessions*
Benedict's *Rule of St Benedict*
Gustavo Gutiérrez's *A Theology of Liberation*
Carole Hillenbrand's *The Crusades: Islamic Perspectives*
David Hume's *Dialogues Concerning Natural Religion*
Immanuel Kant's *Religion within the Boundaries of Mere Reason*
Ernst Kantorowicz's *The King's Two Bodies: A Study in Medieval Political Theology*
Søren Kierkegaard's *The Sickness Unto Death*
C. S. Lewis's *The Abolition of Man*
Saba Mahmood's *The Politics of Piety: The Islamic Revival and the Feminist Subject*
Baruch Spinoza's *Ethics*
Keith Thomas's *Religion and the Decline of Magic*

COMING SOON

Chris Argyris's *The Individual and the Organisation*
Seyla Benhabib's *The Rights of Others*
Walter Benjamin's *The Work Of Art in the Age of Mechanical Reproduction*
John Berger's *Ways of Seeing*
Pierre Bourdieu's *Outline of a Theory of Practice*
Mary Douglas's *Purity and Danger*
Roland Dworkin's *Taking Rights Seriously*
James G. March's *Exploration and Exploitation in Organisational Learning*
Ikujiro Nonaka's *A Dynamic Theory of Organizational Knowledge Creation*
Griselda Pollock's *Vision and Difference*
Amartya Sen's *Inequality Re-Examined*
Susan Sontag's *On Photography*
Yasser Tabbaa's *The Transformation of Islamic Art*
Ludwig von Mises's *Theory of Money and Credit*

The Macat Library By Discipline

Printed in the United States
by Baker & Taylor Publisher Services